Success Starts From The Mind

CONTROL YOUR THOUGHTS

Learn The Proven Strategies To Achieving An Incredibly Productive State of Mind

Mona Yates

Table of Contents

Chapter 1: You're Good Enough 6

Chapter 2: Happy People Find Reasons to Laugh and Forge Deep Connections 9

Chapter 3: 10 Habits to Change Your Life 11

Chapter 4: Happy People Celebrate Other People's Success 18

Chapter 5: *The Daily Routine Experts for Peak Productivity* 20

Chapter 6: Six Habits To Impress Your Boss and Thrive 23

Chapter 7: NOTHING IS IMPOSSIBLE 27

Chapter 8: *7 Reasons Your beliefs Are Holding You Back* 29

Chapter 9: Do The Painful Things First 34

Chapter 10: 10 Habits of Billie Eilish 36

Chapter 11: You Are Going To Be Successful 40

Chapter 12: 10 Habits of Jennifer Lawrence 43

Chapter 13: The Easiest Way to Live a Short, Unimportant Life 47

Chapter 14: *Keep Working When You're Just Not Feeling It* 49

Chapter 15: Happy People Do What Matters to Them 52

Chapter 16: 8 Ways To Deal With Setbacks In Life 54

Chapter 17: 10 Habits That Damage Your Brain 60

Chapter 18: Happy People Surround Themselves with The Right People 65

Chapter 19: 10 habits of Beyoncé 68

Conclusion 71

Chapter 20: Happy People Only Focus on What Is Within Their Control 72

Chapter 21: 10 Reasons Money Can't Buy You Happiness 75

Chapter 22: 8 Habits That Can Make You Happy 81

Chapter 23: Confidence: The Art of Humble-Pride 86

Chapter 24: Become A High Performer 88

Chapter 25: 10 Habits of Kamala Harris 92

Chapter 26: How To Stop Worrying About Failure 96

Chapter 27: How to Learn Faster 100

Chapter 28: 10 Habits of Taylor Swift 103

Chapter 29: 6 Ways To Adopt A Better Lifestyle For Long-Term Success 107

Chapter 30: 5 Ways To Deal with Personal Feelings of Inferiority ... 112

Chapter 31: Happy People View Problems as Challenges 115

Chapter 32: Why Are You Working So Hard 118

Chapter 33: How Successful People Figure What To Focus On 121

Chapter 34: Becoming High Achievers 124

Chapter 1:
You're Good Enough

People come and say 'I did something stupid today. I am so bad at this. Why is it always me?' You will acknowledge even if no one else says it, we often say it to ourselves.

So what if we did something stupid or somewhat a little awkward. I am sure no one tries to do such things voluntarily. Things happen and sometimes we cause them because we have a tendency to go out of our way sometimes. Or sometimes our ways have a possibility of making things strange.

It doesn't make you look stupid or dumb or ugly or less competent. These are the things you make up of yourself. I am not saying people don't judge. They do. But their judgment should not make you think less of yourself.

No matter how much you slip up, you must not stop and you must not bow down to some critique. You only have to be a little determined and content with yourself that you have got it alright.

You need to realize your true potential because no matter what anyone says, you have what it takes to get to the top.

Need some proof? Ask yourself, have you had a full belly today? Have you had a good night's sleep last night? Have you had the will and energy to get up and appear for your job and duties? Have you had the guts to ask someone out to dinner because you had a crush on them?

If you have a good answer to any of these questions, and you have done it all on your own with your efforts. Congratulations my friend, you are ready to appraise yourself.

You have now come to terms with your abilities and you don't need anyone else's approval or appraisal. You don't depend on anyone either psychologically or emotionally.

So now when the times get tough you can remind yourself that you went through it before. And even if you failed back then, you have the right energy and right state of mind to get on top of it now. You are now well equipped to get ahead of things and be a better person than you were the last time.

You are enough for everything good or not so good happening in and around you.

Your health, your relations, your carrier, your future. Everything can be good and better when you have straightened out your relationship with yourself. When you have found ways to talk to yourself ad make yourself realize your true importance. When you learn to admire yourself.

Once you learn to be your best critic, you can achieve anything. Without ever second-guessing yourself and ever trying to care for what anyone else will think.

If you find yourself in a position where you had your heart broken but you still kept it open, you should have a smile on your face. Because now you might be on your path to becoming a superior human being.

Chapter 2:

Happy People Find Reasons to Laugh and Forge Deep Connections

"...Making a connection with men and women through humour, happiness and laughter not only helps you make new friends, but it is the means to establish a strong, meaningful connection to people."

People always try to have a personality that attracts people and makes them feel comfortable around them. Utilizing their humour has been one of those ways to create new friendships. But once you start doing this, you will realize that this humorous nature has emotions and attitudes that comprise happiness and positivity. This will also help you create deep and meaningful connections that will last a lifetime.

When you intend to focus on humour to find deep connections, your subconscious mind starts focusing on positivity. You will slowly turn out to be more positive in your reasoning and conduct because awareness of what's funny is truly only demonstrative of one's very own bliss. In this manner, you're sustaining a more appealing, and that's just the beginning "contagious" attitude. Similarly, as we search out bliss in our everyday lives through satisfying work, leisure activities, individual interests and day to day life, so too do people seek out and wish to be encircled by joy on a relational level: joy and bitterness are contagious, and we as a whole wish to get the happy bug.

Humour helps fashion friendships since we wish to encircle ourselves with individuals who are glad. This way, our objective shouldn't just be to utilize humour to make new companions, however to zero in on the entirety of the uplifting perspectives and feelings that include an entertaining and carefree nature. By embodying satisfaction, inspiration, happiness, receptiveness and tranquillity, we sustain a more grounded and "contagious" state of being.

Historically there was a negative connotation attached to humour, but over the years, research was done, and it proved otherwise. In any case, research on humour has come into the daylight, with humour currently seen as a character strength. Good brain science, a field that analyzes what individuals progress admirably, notes that humour can be utilized to cause others to feel better, acquire closeness, or help buffer pressure. Alongside appreciation, expectation and otherworldliness, a funny bone has a place with the arrangement of qualities positive clinicians call greatness; together, they help us manufacture associations with the world and give significance to life. Enthusiasm for humour corresponds with different qualities, as well, like insight and love of learning. Furthermore, humour exercises or activities bring about expanded sensations of passionate prosperity and idealism.

Once you step into adulthood, it can be difficult for many people to form friendships and then keep up with them because all of us get busier in our lives. Still, it's never too much to go to a bar and strike up a conversation with a random person and believe us, if you have a good sense of humour, they will be naturally attracted towards you.

Chapter 3:
10 Habits to Change Your Life

I'm sure everyone wonders at a certain point in their life that what is the thing that is stopping them from reaching their goals. It is your bad and unhealthy habits that hold you down. If you want to succeed in life, you need to get rid of these habits and adopt healthy habits to help you in the long run.

Here are 10 healthy habits that will change your life completely if you can adopt them in your daily life:

1. Start Following a Morning Ritual

Everyone has something that they love to do, i.e., things that boost their energy and uplifts their mood. Find one for yourself and do that every morning. It will help you kickstart your day with a bright and cheerful mood. It will also help you to eliminate mental fatigue and stress. You will find yourself super energetic and productive. Let me tell you some morning rituals that you can try and get benefitted from.

- *Eating Healthy:* If you are very passionate about health and fitness, eating healthy as a morning ritual might be a win-win situation for you. You can have a nutritious breakfast every morning. Balance your breakfast with proper amounts of carbs, fats, proteins, etc. It will not only help you in staying healthy but will also help you kickstart your day on a proactive note.

- *Meditating:* Meditation is an excellent way of clearing your mind, enhancing your awareness, and improving your focus. You can meditate for 20 to 30 minutes every morning. Then you can take a nice warm shower, followed by a fresh cup of coffee. Most importantly, meditating regularly will also help you strengthen your immune system, promote emotional stability, and reduce stress.

- *Motivating:* A daily dose of motivation can work wonders for you. When you are motivated, your productivity doubles, and you make the best out of your day. Every morning, you can simply ask yourself questions like, "If it is the last day of your life, what do you want to do?", "What productive thing can I do today to make the best out of the day" "What do I need to do in order to avoid regretting later for having wasted a day?". When you ask yourself questions like these, you are actually instructing your brain to be prepared for having a packed-up and productive day.

- *Writing:* Writing can be a super-effective way of kickstarting your day. When you journal all your thoughts and emotions every day after waking up, it allows you to relieve yourself from all the mental clutter, unlocks your creative side, and sharpens your focus.

- *Working Out:* Working out is a great morning ritual that you can follow every day. When you work out daily, it helps you burn more fat, improves your blood circulation, and boosts your energy level. If you are interested in fitness and health, this is the perfect morning ritual for you. You can do some cardio exercises, or some strength training, or both. Depending on your suitability, create a workout routine for yourself and make sure to stick to that. If you don't stick to your routine, it won't be of much help.

-

2. Start Following the 80/20 Rule

The 80/20 rule states that almost 20% of the tasks you perform are responsible for yielding 80% of the results. It is why you should invest more time in tasks that can give you more significant results instead of wasting your time on tasks that yield little to no results. In this way, you can not only save time but also maximize your productivity. Most importantly, when you see the results after performing those tasks, you will be more motivated to complete the following tasks. After you have finished performing these tasks, now you can quickly move your concentration and focus towards other activities that you need to do throughout your day.

3. Practice Lots of Reading

Reading is a great habit and a great way to stimulate your creativity and gaining more knowledge. When you get immersed in reading, it calms you and improves your focus, almost similar to meditating. If you practice reading before going to bed, you are going to have a fantastic sleep. You can read non-fiction books, which will help you seek motivation, develop new ideas, and broaden your horizon. You can also get a lot of advice about how to handle certain situations in life.

4. Start Single-tasking

Multitasking is hard, and almost 2% of the world's total population can do this properly. You can try multitasking occasionally. If you keep on trying to do this all the time, it will form a mental clutter, and as a result, your brain won't be able to filter out unnecessary information. Many studies have suggested that it can severely damage your cognitive control and lower your efficiency when you multitask a lot. It is the main reason why you should try to do single-tasking more than multitasking. Prepare a list of all the tasks you need to perform in a day and start with the most important one. Make sure not to rush and to complete one thing at a time.

5. Start Appreciating More

Appreciating things is totally dependent on your mentality. For example, some people can whine and complain about a glass being half empty, whereas some people appreciate that there is half a glass of water. It totally depends on your point of view and way of thinking. People get blinded by the urge to reach success so much that they actually forget to appreciate the little things in life. If you are working and earning a handsome salary, don't just sit and complain about why you are not earning more, what you need to do to achieve that, etc. You should obviously aim high, but not at the cost of your well-being. When you practice gratitude, it increases your creativity, improves your physical health, and reduces your stress. You can start writing about the things you are grateful for in your journal every day before going to bed, make some time for appreciating your loved ones, or remind yourself of all the things you are grateful for before going to bed every day. If you are not happy with your current situation, you will not be happy in the future. You need to be happy and satisfied at first, and then only you can work on progressing further.

6. Always Keep Positive People Around You

When you have toxic people around you, it gets tough for you to stay in a good mood or achieve something good in life. Toxic people always find a way to pull you down and make you feel bad about yourself. You should always surround yourself with people who are encouraging and positive. When you do that, your life is going to be full of positivity.

7. Exercise on a Regular Basis

Start exercising regularly to maintain good health and enhancing your creativity and cognitive skills. It also increases your endurance level and boosts your energy. When you exercise regularly, your body produces more endorphins. These hormones work as anti-depressants.

8. Start Listening More

Effective communication is very important in maintaining both professional and personal relationships. For communicating effectively, you need to work on your listening capability first. You need to pay attention to the things said by others instead of focusing only on what you have to say. Listening to others will allow you to understand them better. When you listen to someone, it makes them understand that they are valued and that you are here to listen to them. When they feel important and valued, they also start paying attention to what you say, thereby contributing to effective communication. Don't try to show fake concentration while you are busy thinking about something else. When you listen more, you learn more.

9. Take a Break from Social Media (Social Media Detox)

Many studies have shown that excessive use of social media can contribute to depression. Most importantly, it wastes a lot of time because people meaninglessly scroll, swipe, and click for hours. It is a very unhealthy habit and is very bad for bothe physical and mental health. Sometimes you need to completely stop using social media for a while to reduce mental clutter and stress. Turn off your laptops and phones every day for a few hours. It will help you to reconnect with the surrounding world and will uplift your mood.

10. Start Investing More in Self-care

Make some time for yourself out of your busy schedule. It is going to boost your self-esteem, improve your mental health, and uplift your mood. You need to do at least one thing for yourself every day that will make you feel pampered and happy. You can prepare a mouth-watering meal, take a comfortable bubble bath, learn something new, or just relax while listening to music.

The moment you start introducing these habits in your daily, you will instantly see change. Remember that even a tiny step towards a positive change can give outstanding results if you stay consistent.

Chapter 4: Happy People Celebrate Other People's Success

What a phony smile... Why do people want him? How has he accomplished anything? It's ME they need. I'm the one who should be successful, not him. What a joke." This was my inner dialogue when I heard about other people's success. Like a prima donna, I seethed with jealousy and couldn't stand to hear about people doing better than me.

But all the hating got me nowhere. So I thought about who I was really mad at...it wasn't the successful people I raged at. When I got more serious about succeeding, I channeled that useless envy into accepting myself.

I practiced self-acceptance with a journal, through affirmations, and by encouraging myself—especially when I failed. Then something weird happened. I started feeling happy for other people's success. Without a hint of irony, I congratulated people on their hard work, and I applauded their success with my best wishes. It felt good. I felt more successful doing it.

> "Embrace your uniqueness. Time is much too short to be living someone else's life." – Kobi Yamada

My writing career caught fire at the same time. I was published on sites that I'd only dreamt of, and whose authors I had cussed for doing things that the egotistical me still hadn't. Congratulating others started a positive feedback loop. The more I accepted myself, the more I celebrated other people's success and the more I celebrated their success, the more success I achieved. Now that I look back, I could've hacked my growth curve by celebrating others' success as a daily ritual.

1. **It conditions you for your own success**

Feeling good for someone else's success helps you generate the same feelings you need for your own accomplishments. So put yourself in the other's shoes. Revel in their accomplishments; think of all the hard work that went into it. Celebrate their success and know that soon you'll experience the same thing for yourself. Apply the good feelings to your visions for a brighter future.

2. **You'll transcend yourself**

Everyone knows that to actually succeed, you need to be part of something bigger. But most people are kept from that bigger something by wanting all the focus for themselves. it's an ego issue.

Through celebrating others, you'll practice the selflessness it takes to let go of your tiny shell and leap into the ocean of success that comes through serving others. Cheer your fellow entrepreneurs. Feel their success. Let go of your want for recognition and accept that you'll get it when you help enough other people.

Chapter 5:

The Daily Routine Experts for Peak Productivity

What is the one thing we want to get done for a successful life? That is an effective daily routine to go through the day, every day. History is presented as an example that every high achiever has had a good routine for their day. Some simple changes in our life can change the outcome drastically. We have to take the experts' advice for a good lifestyle. We have to choose everything, from color to college, ourselves. But an expert's advice gives us confidence in our choice.

You have to set the bar high so that you get your product at the end of the day. Experts got their peak productivity by shaping their routine in such a way that it satisfies them. The productivity expert Tim Ferriss gave us a piece of simple yet effective advice for such an outcome. He taught us the importance of controlling oneself and how essential it is to provide yourself with a non-reactive practice. When you know how to control yourself, life gets more manageable, as it gives you the power to prevent many things. It reduces stress which gets your productivity out.

Another productive expert of ours, Cal Newport, gives us his share of information. He is always advising people to push themselves to their limits. He got successful by giving his deep work more priority than other work. He is managing multitasks at the same time while being a husband and a father. He is a true example of a good routine that leads to positive productivity. It would help if you decided what matters to you the most and need to focus on that. Get your priorities straight and work toward those goals. Construct your goals and have a clear idea of what your next step will be. It will result in increasing your confidence.

Now, the questions linger that how to start your day? Early is the answer. Early to bed and early to rising has been the motto of productive people. As Dan Ariely said, there is a must 3 hours in our day when our productivity is at its peak. A morning person hit more products, as it's said that sunrise is when you get active. Mostly from 8 o'clock to 10 o'clock. It's said that morning is the time when our minds work the sharpest. It provides you alertness and good memory ability. It is also called the "protected time." We get a new sense to think from, and then we get a sound vision of our steps and ideas to a routine of peak productivity.

Charles Duhigg is a known news reporter, works for the New York Times. He tells us to stop procrastinating and visualizing our next step in life. Not only does it give you confidence, but it also gives you a satisfactory feeling. You get an idea of the result, and you tend to do things more that way. This way, you get habitual of thinking about your next step beforehand. Habits are gradually formed. They are difficult to change but easy to assemble. A single practice can bring various elements from it. Those elements can help you learn the routine of an expert.

You will eventually fall into place. No one can change themselves in one day. Hard work is the key to any outcome. Productivity is the result of many factors but, an excellent daily routine is an integral part of it which we all need to follow. Once you fall into working constantly, you won't notice how productive you have become. It becomes a habit. There might be tough decisions along the way, which is typical for an average life. We need to focus on what's in front of us and start with giving attention to one single task on top of your priority list. That way, you can achieve more in less time. These are some factors and advice to start a daily routine for reaching the peak of productivity with the help of some great products.

Chapter 6:
<u>Six Habits To Impress Your Boss and Thrive</u>

It is still unclear to a majority of people what their bosses and employers want from them. Some expressly make it crystal to their employees their expectations of them while others are reserved. What is clear though, is that bosses worldwide have a common goal – to make a profit. It is the major reason why they hired people in their companies to work for them. Many employees wrongly believe that unless their superiors make a complaint against them, then their work is satisfactory. This notion is a fallacy. Satisfactorily is not the threshold of competency but uniqueness and creativity.

Here are six common habits to impress your boss and thrive:

1. <u>Be Unique And Creative</u>

The question employees fail to answer honestly is what they bring to the table. What is it that makes you stand out in the company you work for? It is not your education level because there are many qualified learned people with your skills. Neither is it the duration you work in the company because you receive remuneration for it.

You should be creative in your work and add value to the company. Your devotion to your work will impress your boss because it is uncommon.

Ideally, you ought to be irreplaceable in your workplace for you to gain favor and earn a promotion.

2. Ensure Proper Communication

Communication is the master key to unlocking conflicts and misunderstandings at the workplace. It is important to ensure proper communication with your boss in your working relationship. You will be able to explain yourself and raise any pertinent issue that affects your work if you have good communication with them.

When you communicate effectively, your superiors will understand you better than if you have poor communication skills or none at all. It may come out as rudeness or ignorance when you communicate ineffectively with your boss. To thrive and gain favor with him/her, build on your communication.

3. Never Outshine Your Master

In his famous book, *48 laws of power*, Robert Greene writes this as his first law. It is prudent never to outshine your master and instead let him appear smarter than you are even if it may not be the case. This speaks life to the respect of hierarchy between your boss and yourself. Never make him appear dumb or lame duck by attracting glory to yourself.

Honor your boss both in your speech and in your actions. This will make you find favor in their eyes and you will thrive in your workplace. It does not imply that you should not give any smart suggestions to your bosses but you should do it in a manner that does not usurp their authority.

4. <u>Have Integrity</u>

Integrity is the quality of honesty and transparency that one may have. You are misplaced and out of order if your boss cannot trust you to do a task without supervision. Worse is that you are in a bad light if you fall short of honesty and cannot be trusted with the management of resources.

Leaders and bosses are universally interested in people of integrity who will fairly work for them. They want people they will trust to oversee the rest and take their organizations to the next level. The lack of integrity is the biggest turn-off for bosses no matter how qualified employees could be. Uphold integrity to impress your boss and you shall thrive.

5. <u>Share Their Vision For The Company</u>

The hiring of managers is tedious and sometimes the competent candidates could not be having the passion of the business at heart. Their remunerations could be their greatest motivation. Routine checks and job evaluations could reveal such hidden traits in employees.

Nevertheless, you need to share the vision of the company with your employer for them to trust you with their resources. People who share the company vision impress hiring managers and owners because their salary is not the sole motivation to work.

6. <u>Be Punctual</u>

It is prudent to be punctual in your job. Punctuality is the act of being on time, never late for anything. You should report to work on time, complete assigned tasks on time, and even submit reports required from you on time.

Being punctual is a sign of dedication to your job. This act alone will make your boss have a soft spot for you.

In conclusion, when you develop these six habits, you will impress your boss and thrive at your workplace.

Chapter 7:
NOTHING IS IMPOSSIBLE

Success is a concept as individual as beauty is, in the eye of the beholder, but with each individuals success comes testing circumstances, the price that must be paid in advance.

The grind,

The pain and the losses all champions have endured.

These hardships are no reason to quit but an indicator that you are heading in the right direction, because we must walk through the rain to see the rainbow and we must endure loss to make space for our new desired results.

Often the bigger the desired change , the bigger the pain, and this is why so few do it.

The very fact that are listening to this right now says to me you have something extra about you.

Inside you know there is more for you and that dream you have, you believe it is possible.

If others have done it before, then so can you , because we can do anything we set our minds and hearts to.

But we must take control of our destiny, have clear results in mind and take calculated action towards those results.

The path may be foggy and unknown but as you commit to the result and believe in it the path, it will be revealed soon enough.

We don't need to know the how, to declare we are going to do something, the how will come later.

Clear commitment to the result is key .

Too many people never live their dreams because they don't know how.

The how can be found out always if we can commit and believe fully in the process.

Faith is the magic elixir to success, without it nothing is possible.

What you believe about you is everything

If you believe you cannot swim and your dream is to be an Olympic swimming champion, what are your chances?

Any rational person would say, well learn to swim,

How many of you want to be multi-millionaires?

I guess everyone?

How many out there know how to get to such a status?

Would we just give up and say it is impossible?

Or would it be as logical as simply learning how to swim or ride a bike?

We believe someone could be an Olympic swimming champion with training and practice , but not a multi-millionaire?

Many of us think big goals are simply too unrealistic.

Fear of failure , fear of what people might think , fear of change , all common reasons for aiming low in life.

But when we aim low and succeed the disappointment in that success is a foul tasting medicine.

Start gaining clarity in the reality of our results.

By thinking bigger we all have the ability to hit what seem now like unrealistic heights, but later realise that nothing is impossible.

We should all start from the assumption that we can do anything, it might take years of training but we can do it. Anything we set our minds to, we can do it.

So ask yourself right now those very important questions.

What exactly would I be doing right now that will make me the happiest person in the world? How much money do I want ?

What kind of relationships do I want?

When You have defined those things clearly,

Set the bar high and accept nothing less.

Because life will pay you any price.

But the time is ticking, you can't have it twice.

Chapter 8:
7 Reasons Your beliefs Are Holding You Back

You know that you have immense potential in your heart, and you are also working hard to attain your desired results, but something still doesn't fit right. Your beliefs might be consciously or unconsciously sabotaging your potential through your actions. This might create the less-than-desirable results that are holding you back from your real success.

Here are some 5 beliefs that might be getting in your way. Observe and analyze them, and start getting rid of them so that your path to success becomes easy and thorn-free.

1. **Beliefs Are More Powerful Than You Think**

"Beliefs have the power to create and the power to destroy. Human beings have the awesome ability to take any experience of their lives and create a meaning that disempowers them or one that can literally save their lives." - Tony Robbins. To change our lives, we first have to change our mindset and what we believe in so dearly. Challenging your beliefs is the key element to improve yourself. If we look around us, we might find a few limiting beliefs in the blink of an eye.

2. **Everyone will get ahead of me if I rest.**

This is perhaps the most crucial limiting belief that the majority of people go through. Many of us think that if we take some time off for ourselves, we'll fall behind in life, and everyone will get ahead of us, crushing us beneath them. For this particular reason, we stop focusing on our needs and necessities and burns out all of our energy on things that should come as second on our lists. Instead, we should convert our "shoulds" into "musts" and focus on ourselves too. Meditating for an hour, going to the gym, taking some time off for hanging out with friends or watching a movie alone, reading a book that's not connected to your work, these all are necessary to sustain life. Making excuses for not taking any time off for yourself and working day and night tirelessly will drain your energy or become a problem for your health; likewise, you will be tired physically and mentally and wouldn't be able to do your tasks on time.

3. Everyone is succeeding in life but me.

With the increasing social media norms and the lives of celebrities on every cover page, or seeing everyone around you figuring their lives out and enjoying themselves, you might feel that you are the only one who hasn't got a thing right. Unfortunately, human nature shows the world our successes and happiness rather than telling them our weak, struggling phases and vulnerability. Comparing yourself to those around you or any celebrity or influencer from social media may become a downward spiral for you when you are feeling confused and lost. Believing that everyone has it easy and you are the only one struggling could make you feel demotivated and depressed. This would, in turn, make you lazy, and you would eventually stop working towards your goal and passion.

4. **I can never be good enough.**

This limiting belief is the most common one among the people. Initially, they would give their all to a new job, a new relationship, or a new task. Then, if things wouldn't work out for them, they would just blame their performance and themselves and would label it as "I'm not good enough for this." This often leads to being anxious and finding perfection in things. And if failed to achieve this, one starts to procrastinate, thinking that their energies and efforts will eventually go to waste anyway. The little voice inside your head telling you that you're not good enough might also make you believe that you're not skilled enough or talented enough for the job or not deserving enough to be with the person you like. As a result, you pull yourself back and miss out on any opportunities offered to you.

5. **I am capable enough to do everything myself.**

We're often fooled by the idea that we don't need anyone's help, and we can figure out everything independently. This approach is majorly toxic as we all need a helping hand now and then. No one walks on the path of success alone. You may feel ashamed or guilty in asking for help or may think that you will be rejected or let down, or may think of yourself as the superior creature who knows everything and are not ready to listen to anyone else. All this might bring you down at one point in your life. We should always be open to any criticism and feedback and should never shy away from asking any help or advice from the people we trust and from the people we get inspired from.

6. The tiny voice becomes too loud sometimes

Limiting beliefs does impede us in some way. There's always this tiny voice in the back of our heads that keeps whispering thoughts and ideas into our minds. Most of what the voice tells us are negative stuff, and the worst part is that we actually start to believe in all of that. "You can never lose weight; stop trying. You're unattractive, and you won't find your significant other any time soon. You don't have the mindset or money to start up your own business; get yourself a 9-5 job instead." All of these, and much more, are what pulls us back from the things that we want to say or the stuff that we want to do.

7. The time isn't right.

The time isn't right, and believe me, it never will be. You're wasting your life away thinking that you will get married, lose your weight, learn a new skill, start your own business, all when the time will be correct. But there's no such as the right time. You either start doing what you want or sit on the side-lines and watch someone else do it. The right time is here and now. It would be best if you started doing the things you want until you make up your mind that you want to do it. You don't have to wait for a considerable amount of money to start a business; start with a small one instead. You don't have to settle down first to get married; find someone who will grow with you and help you. You don't need to spend hours and hours in the gym to lose weight; start eating healthy. There is no right time for anything, but the time becomes right when you decide to change yourself and your life for the better.

Conclusion:

You can make a thousand excuses or find a million experiences to back up your beliefs, but truth be told, you should always be aware of the assumptions you are creating and how they may be affecting your life. For example, will your beliefs stop you from taking action towards your life? Or will you change them into new and creative opportunities to get the results you want?

Chapter 9:

Do The Painful Things First

There are a lot of secret recipes to be happier; one of them is; seek what's painful first. Sure, this may sound a little ironic, but you will be surprised to know that all scientific research is behind this. Behavioral scientists discovered that one of the most effective ways to create an enjoyable experience is to stack the painful parts of the experience early in the process. For example, if you're a doctor, a lawyer, accountant, etc., it's better to break bad news first and then finish with the good news. This will give the clients a more satisfying experience since you start poorly then end on a solid note instead of starting well and ending badly.

There's a couple of crucial reasons why we should do the painful things first. We know that we have limited willpower during the day, and we also know that the most painful activities or tasks are sometimes the most difficult ones. So if we complete the things we find the most difficult first, we'll be exerting less energy on less complicated activities for the rest of the day. Scientific studies show that our prefrontal cortex (creative part of the brain) is the most active the moment we wake up. At the same time, the analytical parts of our brain (the editing and proofreading parts) become more active as the day goes on.

Another reason to do the painful activities firsthand after you wake up is that you would be freed from all the distractions and tend to do these tasks more quickly. If you delay the complex tasks, it will only come back to bite you. Starting with only one task for a day can be enough, as it could lead you to achieve more of them as time goes by. Things like building a new business, losing weight, or learning a new skill require pain and slow work in the beginning to get momentum. But after some persistence, you will likely see your improvements. Behavioral psychology suggests that we're more likely to lead a happier life if we're making improvements over time. Anthony Robbins once said, "If you're not growing, you're dying."

Making slow but gradual improvements is where persistency comes in. It's going to be painful and frustrating initially, and you won't learn a new language in an instant, or your business won't thrive immediately. But when you decide to sacrifice your short-term pleasure for a future pay-off, you will get to enjoy the long-term benefits over a sustained period. Stop avoiding what's hard; embrace it for your long-term happiness.

Chapter 10:

10 Habits of Billie Eilish

Billie Eilish Pirate Baird O'Connell is a Los Angeles-based songwriter, model, and famous singer. Her breakthrough came when her hit song "Ocean Eyes" was uploaded to SoundCloud, an audio-streaming website, in 2016. She has completely disrupted the music industry at 19, captivating the world with her dark and ominous songs.

Eilish has seven Grammy Awards, one Guinness World Record, three MTV Video Music Awards, and two Brit Awards to her credit. She is the youngest artist in Grammy history to win four general field awards in the same year. Music insiders believe Billie and her legions of young fans have the potential to save the music industry—but her success has come at a cost.

Here are the ten habits of Billie Eilish.

1. Delete Negativity

Being famous has its drawbacks, this make Billie Eilish gloomy most of the time. She had to deal with negativity and self-esteem issues because of her body image; however, the love and support from fans and family changed her perspective away from negativity. Ignore the negatives and take care of your mental health!

2. Never Give Up

It's tough when you're constantly depressed and making music. Eilish's music speaks to so many people because it comes from a dark place where many people are right now. Her message to her fans is never to give up, even when your days get harder.

3. Work on Impressing Yourself

Focus on impressing yourself rather than others. All you have is yourself, and how you feel about yourself is all that matters. Speaking to Ssense, Billie said that she wasn't looking forward to impressing the world just to conform to what people want and like. Impressing yourself means being true to the real you.

4. Dance As if No One's Watching

Billie Eilish dances as if no one is looking. Her outlandish and upbeat moves make you want to let go as well. It is so easy to be preoccupied with what others think that you forget to see the good in small things. Live in the present moment and pursue what you truly desire.

5. Focus on Things You're Passionate About

Billie said in an interview that she developed love for music after watching her parents and brother thrive in the music industry. You may not be as fortunate as Billie to have talented parents and siblings to guide and show you the way. But you should find something you enjoy doing and then find mentors who enjoy doing the same thing to show you the way.

6. Rethink Your Marketing Strategies

It is safe to say that Billie Eilish's marketing is out of the ordinary. For instance, she prefers Spotify than the old marketing methods when promoting her music. Who wouldn't want a multisensory experience while listening to a beautiful song? You have to be a little insane to be a good marketer.

7. Stay True to Your True Self

Billie Eilish's unapologetic honesty in her music and how she presents herself is a big part of her appeal. She dresses in baggy clothes and sings about darker topics. Billie stated in an interview that she likes glorifying what makes people uncomfortable. Such a personality will give you an edge over other people.

8. Take Complete Control

Being in control of your destiny shows that you have identified your internal locus of control. It implies accepting responsibility for your thoughts and actions, as well as the consequences. Nothing gets done with Eilish approval, from directing her music videos to promoting her albums.

9. Control Your Self-Worth

When Billboard asked Eilish what advice she would give to women struggling to find their self-worth, she said that it comes from within oneself, and not from people validation. If you don't believe you're worth it, it'll ruin everything. It doesn't matter what anyone else thinks; it's only you who and your opinion matters.

10. Set a good example

Even before Billie came out publicly on body positivity, some parents saw her as a positive role model for young, impressionable listeners. When her career kicked in, she couldn't be seen in a sexy outfit which many saw as appropriate for her age. She then went on to write anti-drug lyrics. You are an excellent leader if your actions leave a legacy that inspires others become more.

Conclusion

Girls and women with differing opinions, such as Billie, are frequently scrutinized, if not despised. And just like Eilish, you can shine through the negativity as long as you know your worth.

Chapter 11:
You Are Going To Be Successful

If you're listening to this ,

chances are you are going to be successful.

Not because this speech is remarkable

or contains information that will definitely change your life.

More because you have begun to do what

less than 20 percent of the population do.

You have begun to look for answers on how to improve your life.

Whether you find that right now

during this speech or in 6 moths from another,

or from a book or video.

If you persist you will find your answers,

and if applied, become successful.

It all depend on the action you take, but as always in life,

you are in control of everything - your thoughts and actions included.

You are infinitely more powerful than you currently believe.

You have capabilities in computing information

that even today's advanced technology doesn't come close to.

You know things that you don't know you know.

Many of your answers will come from inside you.
You beat the odds of 1 in 140 billion just to be born.
You were born as a defenceless baby that could not walk,
talk or even chew food.
But you have evolved into a powerful soul capable of enacting
change on a global scale if you just put your mind to it.

In your life you have learned countless bits of information.
You can be successful if you don't quit.
If you can take it, you can make it.

Take more than you currently believe.
You will make it, and then make it to something
bigger than you can yet comprehend.
You will make it through with belief, persistence, and faith,
just as with every powerful figure of history that
has impacted the world before you.
Every major human achievement in history starts with one person.
It starts with one dream.

The people who are closest to you will probably doubt you.
They probably tell you that it is a pipe dream and that you
should get a normal job and accept your life as it is.
Take everything they say with a pinch of salt.
They might be trying to protect you from disappointment but you know better.

You know the ultimate disappointment would be never trying and never following your dreams.
You know you can do more, have more, and help more.

To those with a vision, doing anything that doesn't contribute to that vision is a waste of time.
Don't let anyone tell you that you can't do something.
If you have that vision you are built to do this.
You shall not and will not accept anything less.

Bet on yourself because someone else's opinion
of you does not have to become your reality.
If you can believe in your success see it and feel
it as if it is real now.
It will not be long before it becomes so.

See it in your mind, believe, and feel it in your heart.
Set out in confidence from the start.
No matter the setbacks or failures,
never quit, and never admit defeat.

Get back on your feet and dust off your shoulder
because it is not over until you succeed or choose to give up.
The choice is yours, and always has been.
You are capable of climbing any mountain if you keep walking despite of the altitude and bad weather on the way to the top.

Chapter 12:
10 Habits of Jennifer Lawrence

Jennifer Lawrence is one of Hollywood's most famous actress, thanks to her role in films such as "The Hunger Games" and "Silver Linings Playbook." But, before her tremendous success, Lawrence struggled to build a name for herself as an actress and model in New York, where she moved when she was 14 years old. After breaking out as the tough-as-nails teenager Ree in the 2010 indie drama "Winter's Bone," Lawrence went on to star in multiple "X-Men" films and drama such as "American Hustle."

I can't think of anyone who doesn't adore Jennifer Lawrence. What is it about this actress that makes her so appealing? It's easy to list a thousand reasons to admire Jennifer Lawrence -from her incredible skill to her quick-witted humour- but honestly, the life lessons she attracts everyone to her.

Here are 10 life habits that Lawrence offers as lessons simply by being herself.

1. Strive for Health and Strength

"I'm never going to starve myself for a part," she declared on the cover of Elle in December 2012. "I don't want little girls to think, 'Oh, I want to look like Katniss; hence I'll skip meals.'" When you're trying to get your physique to appear just suitable, Emma on the other end is trying to make her body appear muscular and robust rather than skinny.

2. Refresh Yourself

How many times has Lawrence stumbled? That's what probably comes to your mind every time you see her trip over the hem of her gown at an awards presentation. Can anyone blame the girl for this? Those outfits appear to be impossible to walk in! But she trips, and every time, without fail, she gets back up and continues walking.

3. Accept Responsibility for Your Mistakes

Lawrence's awkward moments are all the more endearing because she is always the first to laugh at how clumsy she is when she stands. Remember when she collapsed at the 2013 Academy Awards? Or when she collapsed on the red carpet of the 2014 Academy Awards? What does it matter? We're all human, and J. Law never tries to hide it by acting cool and so should you.

4. The Truth Will Set You Free

Even if your truth seems to hurt more, such as that you pee very quickly or that your breasts are unequal, J. Law says that it is what it is, and to be anything other than herself isn't allowed. Embrace your flaws!

5. Look Past the Hype

Remember to key in what's genuine and what's not, and to keep your things in perspective, look past those who take themselves too seriously.

6. Maintain An Open Mind

Lawrence told E! News that her acting job will not bind her for the rest of her life. However, she understands that things happen and that people's lives change, and she is prepared to keep an open mind about it. Being open-minded will direct you to break the monotony for future possibilities.

7. Nobody Is Flawless

Can you recall a scene in American Hustle in which Lawrence's character discusses nail polish? Do you remember the nail polish? She claims it's the smell that keeps drawing her back since it's delicious on the outside but rotten on the inside. Not only is it a beautiful moment, but the discussion is a metaphor for everyone's good and evil sides. Nobody is flawless, and no one loves it when others claim to be.

8. Humility

During a BBC Radio 1 interview, Lawrence remarked her involvement in "The Hunger Games," where she genuinely adores watching the movies she makes because she gets to see how much of a troll, bad, and untalented is. Weird! Indeed, you wouldn't agree with her right? Bu she's adorable because she is humble.

9. Maintain a Sense of Humour

During an interview with Vogue, Lawrence sense of humour could be seen when she cracked a joke on how seeing 13-year olds give her nightmares. She effortlessly doesn't take life too seriously.

10. Love Your Body

Lawrence has spoken out numerous times about her body, challenging unrealistic beauty standards. She claimed in an interview with FLARE magazine that she would rather appear overweight on camera (and appear normal) than diet only to dress like a scarecrow. That is a whole lot of body positivity just for you!

Conclusion

Jennifer will teach you profound truths- when she acts, and when she put on a mask that conceals who she truly is. She given up none of her power by leaving the covers on the screen and refusing to act to "fit in" with Hollywood culture.

Chapter 13:
The Easiest Way to Live a Short, Unimportant Life

An essential and successful life may seem intriguing but, sometimes it's just a lot of work. Whereas, in comparison, a short and unimportant life seems easier to live. The one reason for this may be that you need to eat up your surroundings. People who donate to this world live longer. So, you don't donate. You consume the world. But there is no doubt that people who live longer have many advantages, whereas someone living a short life would not have time for that. Not only is it a loss, but it will affect your life in which you are breathing already.

Few things can lead a person to an unimportant and unhealthy lifestyle. Of course, no one can control how many days we will live on this planet but, we can contribute to our surroundings. And even if you come up with small things, they can impact your life somehow. Be yourself when it comes to shaping. Don't let this world shape you but yourself. It may not only change your life but, it can also give them the confidence to others to change their lives.

It would help if you believed that you could live. If you give up on your life, life will give up on you. Keep yourself worth running in every factor of life. It would be best if you made yourself feel worth it to keep up with the world. Live a meaningful life by all means. How? By contributing to things, talk with a friend, take a long walk in the mornings, or call the people you care about. Even saying hi to a stranger count as contributing to this world. And small contribution leads towards a more significant source of the outcome.

Talk with yourself about how you are going to live this life, and live, not survive. Thet both are different things. We won't know if tomorrow will be our last day, so we got to live it today as it is. Nowadays, we tend to live our lives by ourselves. We prefer to talk on the phone instead of meeting up. It just leads towards an unhealthy and unimportant life. Meet up if you can. Contribute your ideas or decisions to that plan. Make sure that you work out your best if you want it to be done.

A short and unimportant life may seem easier to live by but, it's non-enjoyable. It's full of disadvantages and losses from every side. Isn't it better to live? To give it all your best? We need to devote most of ourselves to this one life that we got. And live each day to its fullest.

Chapter 14:
Keep Working When You're Just Not Feeling It

How many times in a day do you feel like doing nothing? How many times have you had the feeling of getting exhausted and have no energy or motivation to do anything? Do you want answers to these problems? Let's analyze some things.

What were the last big achievement that made you, your family, and your friends proud? When was the last time you had this urge to do a little more work just for the sake of it? Did you feel sorry for yourself and thought how tired you are? These are the problems!

The things that don't make sense to you right now will become more meaningful and purposeful once you get out of your comfort zone. For that, you must start doing what you failed to do the last time.

These feelings of in-activeness and leisure are not a result of some circumstances but the inner voice of every human being that never sleeps and makes us feel like we cannot do this today.

More than often, a change of self is needed than a change of the scenes surrounding us. This is the major task at hand that most people fail to achieve. But we can never give up. This is in fact the spirit of living. The spirit of keep going even when the hardest times hit.

Your body should be the easiest item for you to train and get a hold of. If you are not even able to do that, then there is very little hope for you to achieve anything ever again.

So put yourself in motion and start creating. Instead of thinking about these wrong feelings that your heart gives out just to get you to sleep one more hour, use your time to get creative with life. You don't deserve a good sleep if you haven't done what was meant to be done today. You don't deserve a long breath of relaxation if you haven't tried hard enough to get out of this rut.

You don't feel like getting the job done because you still have a sense of fear and self-pity that keeps you from giving your creative energies another try.

Human beings are the summary of what they repeatedly do, so excellence can also be a habit once you make changes in your behavior for it.

If an inner voice tells you not to do something because you cannot do it, give it a trailer of what is about to come. You will get things done the very first time, and that voice will never bother you again.

These voices and feelings will make you procrastinate rather than performing those actions for real. This is no good way to use your creative energies, just to think of a beautiful scenario and not actually doing something to be in that scenario someday. And laying low because you don't feel like doing it today is the smallest hurdle to pass to get to that place.

All you need is some self-resilience and self-control and the ability to be the master of your body and I doubt there is anything that can stop you then.

Chapter 15:
Happy People Do What Matters to Them

Think about what you want most out of life. What were you created for? What is your mission in life? What is your passion? You were put on this earth for a reason, and knowing that reason will help you determine your priorities.

I spent a total of four months in the hospital, healing from my sickness. During that time, I spent a lot of time thinking about my purpose in life. I discovered that my purpose is to help you change your lives by focusing on what matters most to you.

1. Create A Plan

Create a plan to get from where you are today to where you want to be. Maybe you need a new job. Maybe you need to go back to school. Maybe you need to deal with some relationship issues. Whatever it is, create a plan that will get you to where you want to be.

While I was in the hospital, I began to draft my life plan. My plan guides all of my actions, helps me focus on my relationships with my wife and daughter, and helps me keep working toward my life purpose. A life plan will help you focus your life too.

2. Focus On Now

Stop multitasking and focus on one thing at a time. It may be a project at work. It may be a conversation with your best friend. It may just be the book that you have wanted to read for months. The key is to focus on one thing at a time.

I plan each day the night before by picking the three most important tasks from my to-do list. In the morning, I focus on each one of these tasks individually until they are completed. Once I complete these three tasks, I check email, return phone calls, etc.

3. **Just Say "No."**

We all have too much to do and too little time. The only way you will find the time for the things that matter is to say "no" to the things that don't.

I use my purpose and life plan to make decisions about the projects and tasks I say yes to. If a project or task is not aligned with my purpose, a good fit with my life plan, and sometimes that I have time to accomplish, I say no to the project. Saying no to good opportunities gives you time to focus on the best opportunities.

Research tells us that 97 percent of people are living their life by default and not by design. They don't know where their life is headed and don't plan what they want to accomplish in life.

These steps will help you to decide what matters most to you. They will help you to begin living your life by design and not by default. Most importantly, they will help you to create a life focused on what matters to you.

Let me end by asking, "What matters most to you?

Chapter 16:
8 Ways To Deal With Setbacks In Life

Life is never the same for anyone - It is an ever-changing phenomenon, making you go through all sorts of highs and lows. And as good times are an intrinsic part of your life, so are bad times. One day you might find yourself indebted by 3-digit figures while having only $40 in your savings account. Next day, you might be vacationing in Hawaii because you got a job that you like and pays $100,000 a year. There's absolutely no certainty to life (except passing away) and that's the beauty of it. You never know what is in store for you. But you have to keep living to see it for yourself. Setbacks in life cannot be avoided by anyone. Life will give you hardships, troubles, break ups, diabetes, unpaid bills, stuck toilet and so much more. It's all a part of your life.

Here's 8 ways that you might want to take notes of, for whenever you may find yourself in a difficult position in dealing with setback in life.

1. Accept and if possible, embrace it

The difference between accepting and embracing is that when you accept something, you only believe it to be, whether you agree or disagree. But when you embrace something, you truly KNOW it to be true and accept it as a whole. There is no dilemma or disagreement after you have embraced something.

So, when you find yourself in a difficult situation in life, accept it for what it is and make yourself whole-heartedly believe that this problem in your life, at this specific time, is a part of your life. This problem is what makes you complete. This problem is meant for you and only you can go through it. And you will. Period. There can be no other way.

The sooner you embrace your problem, the sooner you can fix it. Trying to bypass it will only add upon your headaches.

2. Learn from it

Seriously, I can't emphasize how important it is to LEARN from the setbacks you face in your life. Every hardship is a learning opportunity. The more you face challenges, the more you grow. Your capabilities expand with every issue you solve—every difficulty you go through, you rediscover yourself. And when you finally deal off with it, you are reborn. You are a new person with more wisdom and experience.

When you fail at something, try to explore why you failed. Be open-minded about scrutinizing yourself. Why couldn't you overcome a certain situation? Why do you think of this scenario as a 'setback'? The moment you find the answers to these questions is the moment you will have found the solution.

3. Execute What You Have Learnt

The only next step from here is to execute that solution and make sure that the next time you face a similar situation, you'll deal with it by having both your arms tied back and blindfolded. All you have to do is remember what you did in a similar past experience and reapply your previous solution.

Thomas A. Edison, the inventor of the light bulb, failed 10,000 times before finally making it. And he said "I have not failed. I just found 10,000 ways that won't work".

The lesson here is that you have to take every setback as a lesson, that's it.

4. Without shadow, you can never appreciate light

This metaphor is applicable to all things opposite in this universe. Everything has a reciprocal; without one, the other cannot exist. Just as without shadow, we wouldn't have known what light is, similarly, without light, we could've never known about shadow. The two opposites identify and complete each other.

Too much of philosophy class, but to sum it up, your problems in life, ironically, is exactly why you can enjoy your life. For example, if you are a chess player, then defeating other chess players will give you enjoyment while getting defeated will give you distress. But, when you are a chess prodigy—you have defeated every single chess player on earth and there's no one else to defeat, then what will you do to derive pleasure? Truth is, you can now no longer enjoy chess. You have no one to defeat. No one gives you the fear of losing anymore and as a result, the taste of winning has lost its appeal to you.

So, whenever you face a problem in life, appreciate it because without it, you can't enjoy the state of not having a problem. Problems give you the pleasure of learning from them and solving them.

5. View Every Obstacle As an opportunity

This one's especially for long term hindrances to your regular life. The COVID-19 pandemic for instance, has set us back for almost two years now. As distressing it is, there is also some positive impact of it. A long-term setback opens up a plethora of new avenues for you to explore. You suddenly get a large amount of time to experiment with things that you have never tried before.

When you have to pause a regular part of your life, you can do other things in the meantime. I believe that every one of us has a specific talent and most people never know what their talent is simply because they have never tried that thing.

6. Don't Be Afraid to experiment

People pursue their whole life for a job that they don't like and most of them never ever get good at it. As a result, their true talent gets buried under their own efforts. Life just carries on with unfound potential. But when some obstacle comes up and frees you from the clutches of doing what you have been doing for a long time, then you should get around and experiment. Who knows? You, a bored high school teacher, might be a natural at tennis. You won't know it unless you are fired from that job and actually play tennis to get over it. So whenever life gives you lemons, quit trying to hold on to it. Move on and try new things instead.

7. Stop Comparing yourself to others

The thing is, we humans are emotional beings. We become emotionally vulnerable when we are going through something that isn't supposed to be. And in such times, when we see other people doing fantastic things in life, it naturally makes us succumb to more self-loathing. We think lowly of our own selves and it is perfectly normal to feel this way. Talking and comapring ourselves to people who are seemingly untouched by setbacks is a counterproductive move. You will listen to their success-stories and get depressed—lose self-esteem. Even if they try their best to advise you, it won't get through to you. You won't be able to relate to them.

8. Talk to people other people who are having their own setbacks in life

I'm not asking you to talk to just any people. I'm being very specific here: talk to people who are going through bad times as well.

If you start talking to others who are struggling in life, perhaps more so compared to you, then you'll see that everyone else is also having difficulties in life. It will seem natural to you. Moreover, having talked with others might even show you that you are actually doing better than all these other people. You can always find someone who is dealing with more trouble than you and that will enlighten you. That will encourage you. If someone else can deal with tougher setbacks in life, why can't you?

Besides, listening to other people will give you a completely new perspective that you can use for yourself if you ever find yourself in a similar situation as others whom you have talked with.

Conclusion

Setbacks are a part of life. Without them we wouldn't know what the good times are. Without them we wouldn't appreciate the success that we have gotten. Without them we wouldn't cherish the moments that got us to where we are heading to. And without them there wouldn't be any challenge to fill our souls with passion and fire. Take setbacks as a natural process in the journey. Use it to fuel your drive. Use it to move your life forward one step at a time.

Chapter 17:
10 Habits That Damage Your Brain

Our brain is the most vital and unrivaled organ in the body. I am talking about the 100 billion-plus brain cells that are responsible for controlling everything that our body does. But, what I find odd is that often, we tend to neglect our brain health over other parts of our body. We work out and are constantly taking care of our body yet we forget about the most important organ that is basically keeping us alive! Most people are seemingly unaware that our brain requires training and exercise too. I bet most of you already know how crucial habits are in shaping you and your life but did you know that some habits even kill your brain cells? What if I told you that you could be damaging your own brain? Yes. You heard me right. We engage in certain habits in our day-to-day lives that are seemingly harmless but have are damaging our brains. Some of these damages that our brain suffers are known to be long-term and even fatal in some cases. Some examples of brain damage are Dementia and Alzheimer's.

If you want to know what these habits are that you might be engaging in, I am going to discuss ten such habits that are damaging your brain without even you noticing that you should immediately remove them from your life.

1. Skipping Breakfast

How frequently do you skip breakfast? Well, most people skip breakfast due to an ongoing diet, to save time, some do not feel hungry in the morning or just because they do not think it is important enough. However, did you know that skipping breakfast actually leads to brain damage? Remember that our body has gone without any food for approximately 8 hours. When we sleep, our body uses the stored-up nutrients. So, therefore, you should always remember to replenish these nutrients so that the brain and the body have enough energy to function properly throughout the day. Similarly, another Japanese study of 80,000 subjects conducted in a period of over 15 years showed that people who skipped breakfast frequently suffered from a stroke and low blood pressure, which is very harmful to the brain. Did you know that not having breakfast lowers the blood glucose level of the brain? So, the next time you decide to pass on your breakfast, think about the damage you are causing to your own brain.

2. Consuming Too Much Sugar

How often do you crave for and indulge in candies and sugary drinks? Well, because another reason that leads to brain damage is when you consume too much sugar. I bet you already know how eating too much sweet stuff can affect your body health drastically, giving you diabetes and obesity. You might be planning to cut off your sugar intake to have that perfect waistline, but another very important reason why you might want to do so is to protect your brain from being undeveloped. Yes, too much sugar hinders your brain's capacity to develop. It is because when you consume a lot of candies and sweets, it disrupts your body's ability to absorb the important nutrients and proteins, which then results in your body not being able to send these to your brain. This makes your brain malnutritioned and stops its development.

3. Smoking

Smoking is probably the most harmful habit that a person might have. All of us already know smoking gives us a ton of diseases related to the heart and lungs, and not to forget cancer. Well, another reason why you should quit smoking starting today is that it brings about a ton of brain-related illnesses too. Did you know that smoking damages your brain membrane and neural viability of your brain that is responsible for balance, coordination, and motor skills? Not only that, smoking thins the cortex of your brain that deals with language, memory, and perception. Smoking is also a major cause of Dementia, Alzheimer's, and even death. It also leads to inflammation of the brain resulting in illnesses such as Multiple Sclerosis. Considering all this information, I would suggest you take quitting smoking more seriously.

4.   Not Getting Enough Sleep

Did you know that sleep is crucial for both our physical and mental health? So, do you sleep enough? Or too much? The number of hours that you sleep has a direct impact on the functioning of your brain. Sleep deprivation is one of the most common things of this generation. But do you know that it can cause your brain to shrink its size? It can lead to serious issues such as depression, extreme daytime drowsiness, impaired memory. Studies have shown that it is only during the deep sleep cycle that the toxins in your brain are released. Even one night of sleep deprivations leads to issues such as not being able to recall new information and dysfunctioning of your brain. You are basically killing your brain cells by not improving your sleeping habits that will result in memory loss.

5.   Covering Your Head When Sleeping

What if I told you that the way you sleep is also known to cause brain damage? You might be wondering how. But if you are among the many that cover their heads while they sleep, you are causing your brain damage. This is because it leads to carbon dioxide buildup as you will be intaking more carbon dioxide than oxygen to your brain. This can even cause you to have Dementia at an early age.

6.   Blasting Music on Your Headphone

While listening to music on your headphones may be convenient, did you know that listening to loud music and not giving your ears a break causes you brain damage? If you are one of those who constantly listen to music, then you should probably give it a little more thought because you are damaging not only your ears but also your brain. Medical experts say that this can lead to hearing problems and also memory loss. Hearing problems are mostly related to brain problems such as loss of brain tissue. So, it is time you adjust your volume and gives your ears a break so that you can preserve your hearing and protect your brain from further damage.

7. Not Drinking Enough Water

Do you have a habit of over-looking your water intake? Because let me tell you that your brain needs an adequate amount of water to function properly, think faster, and focus better. It is no news that our body made up of 70% of water, right? Therefore, water is crucial to the body and the brain. Researchers say that dehydration has immediate effects on the brain. Even 2 hours of a heavy task without proper hydration can lead to disruptive cognitive functions. The brain needs sufficient water to clean out the toxins in our brains and so that it can carry the nutrients and proteins from our body to the brain. So, don't forget to drink enough water starting today!

8. No Exercise

Did you know that exercising not only improves your body but greatly helps in improving the functioning of your brain? So, how frequently do you exercise? You do not necessarily have to follow a rigorous routine or join a gym. It could be a swim in the pool from time to time or a jog in the morning. Exercising increases your heart rate, which then helps pump more oxygen to the brain. With the release of happy hormones known as endorphins, exercising also helps you remain younger. Not only that, but exercising is also known to produce and release other hormones that help the brain to grow and develop.

9. Overeating

Overeating is when you eat more than what your body needs. Eating too much is never a good idea as we all know the terrible consequences it brings about, such as an increase in weight, obesity, and cholesterol, among others. But among all this, did you know that overeating affects your brain too? It makes the arteries of your brains harder, leading to a decrease in mental power. Not only that, it creates an unhealthy cycle of overeating out of boredom, it also disrupts your sleeping habits, all of which cause stress and thus decrease your brain health more.

10. Working When Sick

Do not forget that your brain works the hardest, and so it is vital that you give it a rest. You can never get your brain back to its shape no matter how much you rest after you have overused it. Therefore, whenever you are sick, like having a headache or flu, or even when you are exhausted, do not push your brain to work. This will lead to a decrease in the effectiveness of the brain. If you have a habit of working like this, you are making your brain suffer severe and irreversible damage.

That brings us to the end of the ten habits that damage our brain. If you identified and related to one or more of these habits, then it is time that you remove them completely from your life so that you can preserve your most important body part - the brain, which also means protecting your whole body.

Chapter 18:
Happy People Surround Themselves with The Right People

Whether we realized it or not, we become like the five people we spend the most time with. We start behaving like them, thinking like them, looking like them. We even make decisions based on what we think they would want us to do.

For example, there are many research findings that prove we are more likely to gain weight if a close friend or a family member becomes overweight. Similarly, we are more likely to engage in an exercise program if we surround ourselves with fit and health-oriented people.

So, who are the top 5 influencers in your life? Do they make you feel positive? Do they inspire and motivate you to be the best version of yourself? Do they support and encourage you to achieve your goals? Or, do they tell you that "it can't be done," "it's not possible," "you aren't good enough," "you will most likely fail."

If you feel emotionally drained by the energetic vampires in your life, you may want to detox your life and get rid of the relationships that aren't serving you in a positive way.

The negative people, the naysayers, the Debbie Downers, and the chronic complainers are like a dark cloud over your limitless potential.

They hold you back and discourage you from even trying because they're afraid that if you succeed, you'll prove them wrong.

Have the courage to remove the negative people from your life and watch how your energy and enthusiasm automatically blossom. Letting go of the relationships that aren't serving us is a critical step if we want to become more positive, fulfilled, and successful.

Detoxing your life from negative influencers will also allow you to become the person you truly want to be. You'll free yourself from constant judgment, negativity, and lack of support.

Here's what you can do:

- Stay away from chronic complainers.
- Stop participating in meaningless conversations.
- Share your ideas only with people who are supportive or willing to provide constructive criticism.
- Minimize your interactions with "friends," coworkers, and family members who are negative, discouraging, and bitter.
- Stop watching TV and reading negative posts on social media (yes, mainstream media is a major negative influence in our lives!).
- Surround yourself with positive and successful people (remember, we become like the top 5 people we spend our time with!).

- Find new, like-minded friends, join networking and support groups, or find a positive coach or a mentor.

If you want to make a positive change in your life, remember, the people around you have a critical influence on your energy, growth, and probability of success.

Positive people bring out the best in you and make you feel motivated and happy. They help you when you're in need, encourage you to go after your dreams, and are there to celebrate your successes or support you as you move past your challenges. Pick your top 5 wisely!

Chapter 19:
10 habits of Beyoncé

Beyonce is a renowned Houston-born singer, dancer, songwriter, actor, and businesswoman. She rose to prominence as a member of the pop singing R&B group "Destiny's Child." Beyonce is ultimately life goals; she is always at the top of her game, tries new things (and smashes them), admits her mistakes, balances her family life, and spends time with the people who matter. She always points out on working tirelessly to the top with the help of her mother and father from the age of nine.

How has she managed to win Grammys, make platinum albums, star in many A-list films, run a lucrative clothing line, perfume business, and raising three gorgeous children?

Here are 10 Mrs. Carter habits that you can emulate.

1. Above All, Love Yourself

Beyonce have had a share of work-family balance struggles when raising her three kids. Realizing how overwhelming it can be, she opts for self-love practices that means more rest if need be. You have goals and desires, which is terrific! But it's pointless making all that only to die as soon as you acquire it. Practise self-care.

2. Make the Most of Your Time

Beyonce's advice as a self-made millionaire is not to waste time. If you want to attain your goals, you must respect your time before others do. Everyone, rich or poor, has the same number of hours in a day. But the question is, what are you doing with your 24 hours? Are you making the best use of your time?

3. Keep Your Personal Life a Mystery

Talking to Oprah in an interview, "Queen Bey" said that she is purposefully private because revealing everything deprives her of enjoying her personal life. Your personal life should be sacred because letting everyone in may ruin it.

Beyonce believes that he fans should only be familiar with her through her art and music; the rest she reserves for her family and friends.

4. Love Your Body

Beyoncé is a representation of beauty, power, and health. Beyoncé recently claimed that she has been following a vegan diet, not for weight loss, but to be the best version of herself. Spending time on yourself is crucial, and learning to love yourself is imperative, whether the healthiest version of yourself means giving up meat or simply spending an extra few hours in the gym each month.

5. Be the Best Version of You

If there is one thing we can learn from Beyonce, is that no one will scold you on bringing out your best. Quoting her words in her documentary, "power will never be given to you; you must take it yourself." If you want it big, nobody is going to do it for you. If you are not invited to the table, drag yourself a chair and sit.

6. Take Charge of Your Success

Beyonce is a good example of what economic equality is. She is one who doesn't shy off celebrating her achievements as a woman. Beyonce isn't afraid to flaunt her "paper" and personal accomplishments. She is always proud of her hustle and isn't afraid to exploit her past triumphs to prove her worth. That is how you advance - both professionally and personally.

7. Hard Work Is Recognizable

A "smart person" will frequently imply that good soft skills can compensate for time spent on "the little things." However, Beyonce's stage appearance and performance demonstrates that hard work will be appreciated by those who admire your work, as well as those who don't know you.

8. Opinionated

Beyonce is defined by her beauty and brains. She is an activist on important topics, for instant, her opinions had an influence during Obama's administration, and she also promoted Michelle Obama's efforts to promote humanitarianism. Weigh in your opinion where it matters.

9. Negativity Derails You

Stay away from negativity and concentrate on working hard and doing your best. Beyonce is a challenge to most of her peers in the industry because she does not waste time on frivolous things and the negative people on her pages trying to bring her.

10. Her Priorities

Beyoncé's story revolves around her family, and she frequently emphasizes it as her driving force. Those people who journey with you from scratch to success are the same people who you should credit.

Conclusion

There is nothing powerful than knowing and respecting your worth as well as remaining solid on your money-making journey. Even if you don't have Beyoncé's level of riches, learn to handle your life cautiously.

Chapter 20:
Happy People Only Focus on What Is Within Their Control

We cloud our judgment and lose the sense of our role in shaping our reality.

Such can be the case today.

We're fighting through a global pandemic, and I can assure you every one of us is having good days and bad days.

On the good days, we try to stay positive and be productive. On the bad days, we sulk into the worry of predicting what the future will be like. We imagine it, and then we start living it, which leaves us feeling helpless and scared.

Thoughts fire before emotions—that's why when we think negatively, we feel negative emotions.

But there's a way around this.

Whenever I find myself moving from a positive outlook to a negative one, I try my best to bring my attention back to the most important aspect of all.

I ask myself these three questions:

1. What is worrying me?
2. What is within my control?
3. What matters most to me, and what can I do about it?

When we focus on what we can control, our thoughts empower us and then trigger positive emotions.

Do we give our power away to factors we cannot control, or do we retain it and direct our energy onto the options we can control?

When my mind plays tricks on me and slides me into a stream of worry, I consciously try to swim out of it. And I use this framework below to reorient my thoughts and whisk them up into a more sunny state of mind.

A Sunshine State of Mind

At any given stage in your life, regardless of the set of circumstances you are dealing with, you can find yourself in one of four mental states:

- **Quadrant #1: Wasting your energy.** When you focus on what is not within your control, you're wasting your energy on factors that will not move you forward. This is like having a 2-week vacation booked, which was canceled due to the pandemic. You can complain all you want, but what's the use? Stop draining your energy on it and start thinking clearly.

- **Quadrant #2: Being paranoid.** When you ignore what is not within your control, you're paranoid. You shouldn't ignore external factors, instead, accept what is and be aware of the external conditions that are outside your control. For instance, with this pandemic, we must understand the situation and how it progresses because its advancements have implications on our lives. We don't want to give our undivided attention, but we do want to stay educated on it.

- **Quadrant #3: In a sunshine state of mind.** When you focus on what is within your control, you're in the driver's seat. You're intentional about your attitude and how you spend your energy. This is where you are emotionally mature and thinking rationally and clearly in a sunshine state of mind. And what does it do to you? It keeps you positive, energized, and motivated.

Chapter 21:
10 Reasons Money Can't Buy You Happiness

I'm sure you have heard this statement before, that "Money can't buy happiness.", but have you stopped to think about why it might be so? Many of us chase money and that high paying job because we believe that it will bring us wealth which will in turn make us happy. We do it because it is what society tells us we should be doing. That we should trade all our time and energy to make money no matter how many sacrifices we have to make with regards to our friendships, relationships, and so on.

It is true that a certain income level and money in the bank is required to allow us to have a comfortable standard of living, which could make life quite nice for us. But beyond that, it will be tough to derive happiness from just sheer truckloads of money alone, as we will soon find out.

1. Our Happiness Is Not Derived From Material Things

This is arguably the most important yet easily overlooked aspect when it comes to dealing with money. While most of us will have desires to live in a dream home, owning the ultimate luxury car, and buying the greatest gifts we can buy when we're rich, we fail to realize that the process of acquisition of material things is a futile effort. It is always thrilling to be on the forefront of owning the latest material good on the market, but the excitement you have for a product usually fades away pretty quickly once you have them in your hands. We acclimatize very quickly to what we have, and we search for the next thing almost immediately. This seemingly endless chase for happiness would seem like a carrot on a stick, always dangling it's juiciness in front of you but you never get to taste it. If you look around at the things you have in your house, you will know what I mean. All the stuff that was once intriguing to you now no longer has the same effect of joy and happiness that it once had. Bottom line is that there is no amount of stuff you can acquire that will ever make you truly happy.

2. Money Cannot Buy You Relationships

We fail to realize the power of relationships when it comes to the happiness equation. Happiness can easily be derived from thriving relationships. Relationships that serve to enrich our lives in all aspects of it. When we are in a relationship with someone who loves and cares for us unconditionally, there is no amount of money that can buy you that feeling. The same goes for friendships and family. Having people that support you in your endeavors, grieve with you when you experience loss, or

just someone you can talk to, to share your feelings of excitement, sorrow, and all the different ranges of emotions, those are the moments that truly matter in life.

3. Money Could Lure Disingenuous People

While some may argue that you can buy friendships by paying people to be around you, I am pretty sure most of you wouldn't want to go down that path. You know that these people are not hanging around you because they like you, but because they like what you have in your pocket. Genuine relationships are ones that will last even when you don't have a dime left in your back account. When all else fails, you will want to have these people around you for support.

4. You Will Never Feel Like You have Enough Money

Chasing money as a substitute for happiness is a tricky thing. We all think we need $1 million dollars in our bank account to be happy, but as soon as we hit that milestone, something just doesn't feel quite right. We feel empty inside, we feel like maybe it's not enough, so we set a bigger target of $2 million. But that day will come too and again we will feel like something is amiss. The cycle repeats itself until we finally realize that deriving happiness from a monetary goal is also a futile effort.

5. Money Only Helps To Improve Your Standard of Living

Instead of using money as bait for happiness, use it for what it really is for - survival, food, clothing, a roof over your head, and the occasional splurge on something you like. Beyond that, look elsewhere for happiness. I am here to tell you that it is human nature for us to feel like we never have enough of something, and that includes money. We have been programmed to always want and need more. More of everything. We compare to people more successful than us and think we need to live like them in order to be happy. Don't make the same mistake as everyone else. Find a comfortable amount you need for survival and retirement, and the rest is bonus.

6. Making Money Requires Sacrifices

Unless you're a trust fund baby, or money falls from the sky, or you managed to strike a jackpot, constantly putting money above all else requires time and effort to earn. Working 12 hour shifts, 7 days a week is no easy feat. You will see your youth fly by and your other priorities fall by the wayside. By the time you've earned the desired income of your dreams, you may well find that a few decades have passed and you're standing on top of the mountain, alone, with no one to share that experience with. No one who may be able to travel with you or even spend that money with you. Unless you consciously try for a balanced work-life, you will find it quite a lonesome experience.

7. The Simple Pleasures In Life Doesn't Require That Much Money

Spending time with your family, going out for coffee with friends, having a chill board games night on the weekends with enthusiasts like yourself, you will find that all these activities brings us closer to the emotional world. The emotional and spiritual connection we have with fellow human beings that bring us laughter, joy, sadness, and happiness. We fail to realize that the happiest moments we can create doesn't require that much money. It just requires planning and some food. Stop chasing the dream vacation halfway around the world for happiness. It is underneath you all along.

8. You Lack the Happiness Mindset

Happiness is merely a feeling, and feelings can be created by choice. Money can't fix your emotional problems, it can only buy you therapy. Ultimately, it's your attitude and mindset that determines your level of happiness that you experience. If you always see the glass half empty, no amount of money can make you see the glass as half full.

9. You Don't Feel Grateful for The Things Money Buy You

We take for granted the things we have acquired so far

and only look towards the next shiny object. Being grateful for our hard-earned money has bought us thus far should be our number one priority. Treasure the bed you bought that you can sleep comfortably in, be thankful for the television you have that allows you to stream your favourite shows on demand, be grateful for the roof that houses all these items and protects you from the elements.

10. We Fall into The If-Then Trap of Chasing Money

How many times do you have the thought that the next promotion you receive will be the happiest moment of your life. Or perhaps that your boss will give me a raise if you turn this project in successfully. If we only chase our paychecks rather than chase fulfillment, we are running the wrong race in life.

Remember these important points the next time you work for money. Yes, having money is important, but it should not adversely affect your ability to live a fulfilling life. There are a million other things that are just as equally important if you're chasing happiness.

Chapter 22:
8 Habits That Can Make You Happy

We're always striving for something, whether it's a promotion, a new truck, or anything else. This brings us to an assumption that "when this happens, You'll finally be happy."

While these important events ultimately make us happy, research suggests that this pleasure does not last. A Northwestern University study compared the happiness levels of ordinary people to those who had won the massive lottery in the previous years. It was found that the happiness scores of both groups were nearly equal.

The false belief that significant life events determine your happiness or sorrow is so widespread that psychologists have given it a name- "impact bias." The truth is that event-based happiness is transitory. Satisfaction is artificial; either create it or not. Long-term happiness is achieved through several habits. Happy people develop behaviors that keep them satisfied daily.

Here are eight habits that can make you happy.

1. Take Pride in Life's Little Pleasures.

We are prone to falling into routines by nature. This is, in some ways, a positive thing. It helps conserve brainpower while also providing comfort. However, it is possible to be so engrossed in your routine that you neglect to enjoy the little pleasures in life. Happy people understand the value of savoring the taste of their meal, revel in a great discussion they just had, or even simply stepping outside to take a big breath of fresh air.

2. Make Efforts To Be Happy.

Nobody, not even the most ecstatically happy people, wakes up every day feeling this way. They work harder than everyone else. They understand how easy it is to fall into a routine where you don't check your emotions or actively strive to be happy and optimistic. People who are happy continually assess their moods and make decisions with their happiness in mind.

3. Help other people.

Helping others not only makes them happy, but it also makes you happy. Helping others creates a surge of dopamine, oxytocin, and serotonin, all of which generate pleasant sensations. According to Harvard research, people who assist others are ten times more likely to be focused at work and 40% more likely to be promoted. According to the same study, individuals who constantly provide social support are the most likely to be happy during stressful situations. As long as you don't overcommit yourself, helping others will positively affect your mood.

4. Have Deep Conversations.

Happy people understand that happiness and substance go hand in hand. They avoid gossip, trivial conversation, and passing judgment on others. Instead, they emphasize meaningful interactions. You should interact with others on a deeper level because it makes you feel good, creates emotional connections, and, importantly, it's an intriguing way to learn.

5. Get Enough Sleep.

I've pounded this one too hard over the years, and I can't emphasize enough how important sleep is for enhancing your attitude, focus, and self-control. When you sleep, your brain recharges, removing harmful proteins that accumulate as byproducts of regular neuronal activity during the day. This guarantees that you awaken alert and focused. When you don't get enough quality sleep, your energy, attention, and memory all suffer. Even in the absence of a stressor, sleep loss elevates stress hormone levels. Sleep is vital to happy individuals because it makes them feel good, and they know how bad they feel when they don't get enough sleep.

6. Surround yourself with the right people

Happiness is contagious; it spreads through people. Surrounding yourself with happy people boosts your confidence, encourages your creativity, and is simply enjoyable.

Spending time with negative people has the opposite effect. They get others to join their self-pity party so that they may feel better about themselves. Consider this: if someone was smoking, would you sit there all afternoon inhaling the second-hand smoke? You'd step back, and you should do the same with negative people.

7. Always Stay Positive.

Everyone, even happy people, encounters difficulties daily. Instead of moaning about how things could or should have been, happy people think about what they are grateful for. Then they find the best approach to the situation, that is, dealing with it and moving on. Pessimism is a powerful source of sadness. Aside from the damaging effects on your mood, the problem with a pessimistic mindset is that it becomes a self-fulfilling prophecy. If you expect bad things, you are more likely to encounter horrific events. Gloomy thoughts are difficult to overcome unless you see how illogical they are. If you force yourself to look at the facts, you'll discover that things aren't nearly as awful as you think.

8. Maintain a Growth Mindset.

People's core attitudes can be classified into two types: fixed mindsets and growth mindsets. You believe you are who you are and cannot change if you have a fixed attitude. When you are challenged, this causes problems because anything that looks to be more than you can handle will make you feel despondent and overwhelmed. People with a growth mindset believe that with effort, they can progress. They are happy as a result of their improved ability to deal with adversity. They also outperform those with a fixed perspective because they welcome difficulties and see them as chances to learn something new.

Conclusion

It can be tough to maintain happiness, but investing your energy in good habits will pay off. Adopting even a couple of the habits on this list will have a significant impact on your mood.

Chapter 23:
Confidence: The Art of Humble-Pride

There is a very fine line between confidence and overconfidence, being bold and being belligerent, having authority and having arrogance. It is a line that trips even the most nimble footed, but usually because they have dedicated no clear thoughts on how to manage it. Instead, they follow their gut on how far they can push or how much they should hold back. This is the paradox; you need to be confident. You need self-belief, you need to be assured of your ability and sometimes even certain of what the outcome will be. All of those things are empowering. In the words of Tony Robbins, you have to awaken the giant within. But had Goliath stooped to consider David's sling he would have worn a different helmet. The problem was that Goliath had a belief that he was fully capable of everything just as he was. I like to call it confidence without context, or universal, unanimous support of the self. That is the dangerous kind of confidence that spills over into arrogance. Chess grandmasters will tell you that the moment you assume you will win is the moment you lose. Because that is precisely when you start to make mistakes. You become too focussed on what your next move is that you don't even see theirs. You become so absorbed in your strategy that you fail to account for their plan and the bigger picture. It was confidence without context that made Goliath run straight towards to the flying stone.

Confidence without context is an assumption. And the problem with assumptions is that they go one step beyond the rationality of an expectation. Assumption goes into the fight drunk, having already celebrated the victory. But that leads to its inevitable demise. Expectation remains present, it acknowledges the reality of the situation. Assumption arrives intoxicated, expectation arrives in control. That is the difference. Pride is the greatest antidote to reason, which makes humility its greatest ally. If you want to stay in the fight you need to have both confidence and humility. If you want to stay competitive, if you want to get a promotion, if you want to level up. Whatever it is that you want, I can guarantee that the path to get there is a hopscotch of humility and confidence. Every bold step forward must be followed by a humble one. Note that humility does not take you backwards, it keeps you balanced. You can hop along in arrogance, but you will never last as long or be as strong as the one who keeps an even stride. If you strive for something, then you need to start striding towards it. And the rhythm of your march should beat to the sounds of a two-tone drum. Because confidence without context is like hopping up stairs – you might reach the second floor, but you will never manage the pyramid.

Chapter 24:
Become A High Performer

We were put on this planet because we were meant to be all we could become. Human beings are the sum of their acts and achievements. But not everyone is capable of doing things to their full potential.

Every man's biggest burden is his or her unfulfilled potential.

So what you need to become a high-performing individual in this modern era of competition is to idolize the best of the best.

You will need to understand the real-life features of a successful individual and what you need to do to become one.

If you want to be more successful in your life you need to become obsessive. Start your day with a goal and try your best to achieve it before you head to bed. You don't necessarily need to be on the right path with the first step, but you will find the best route once you have the undefeated will to find that path.

If you want to be more developed in your life you need to sleep effectively. The most successful people have a mantra of high performing routine. They don't sleep more than five hours a day and work seven days a week. They only take one day a week to sleep more just to rejuvenate their brains and body.

If you want to know if you are a high-performing successful person, look into your body language. If you find ease and leisure in everyday tasks, You are surely not standing up to your potential. If you like to sit for a conversation, start to stand. If you like to walk, start running. Get out of your comfort zone and start thinking and acting differently.

The last thing before you start your search for the right path to excellence is to set a goal every day. Increase your creativity by finding new ways to shorten the time of you becoming the better you and finally getting what you deserve.

You will eventually start seeing your life get on the track of productive learning and execution.

Change your way of treating others, especially those who are below you. If you are not a jolly person when you are broke, you can never be a jolly person when you are rich.

Never underestimate someone who is below you. You never know to whom the inspiration might take you. You have to consider the fact that life is ever-changing. Nothing ever stays the same. People never stay where they are for long.

It is the alternating nature of life that makes you keep fighting and pushing harder for better days. That is why you work hard on your skills to become a hearty human with the arms of steel.

Most people live a quiet life of desperation where they have a lot to give and a lot to say but can never get out of their cocoons.

But you are not every other person. You are the most unique soul god has created to excel at something no one has ever thought or seen before.

Start loving yourself. Stop finding faults in yourself. You are the best version of yourself, you just haven't found the right picture to look into it yet.

You want to be a high performer in every aspect of your life, here is my final advice for you.

If you push your limits in even the smallest tasks of your life, if you stretch your mind and imagination, if you can push the rules to your benefit, you might be the happiest and the most successful man humankind has ever seen.

Keep working for your dreams till the day you die. Life opens its doors to the people who knock on it. The purpose of this life is to knock on every door of opportunity and grasp that opportunity before anyone else steps forward.

You won't fulfill your desires till you make the desired effort, and that comes with a strong will and character. So keep doing what you want to never have a regret.

Chapter 25:
10 Habits of Kamala Harris

Kamala Harris smashed the world's record by being the first Black-Asian Woman Vice President of the United States and has held high-level roles early in her career. Her career kicked off as a lawyer and quickly rose to prominence for high-profile handling cases. Her efforts could later land her the position of the district attorney, which elevated her to new heights when she was elected as California Attorney General, and US Senator. With her empathetic, communicative, and leadership style, Kamala Harris exudes an executive presence that makes her an outstanding leader. Moreover, seeing her in a high position, addressing the nation, conveys that women can achieve everything they set their minds to.

Here are 10 Kamala Harris habits that are worth mentioning.

1. Gender Isn't a Limit.

Kamala is an inspiration to women's success in male-dominated fields. Gender, according to her, should not limit you from pursuing your dreams just because they are stereotypically not for you. She believes that both men and women should have equal access to resources for achieving greatness.

2. Make Informed Decisions

The choices you make today will have a significant impact on your future. According to Harris, tackle everything with due diligence. Having served in the public service for many years, she understands the importance of making informed choices or decisions.

3. Family Comes First

Some Professions demand huge sacrifices, which is why you should have your family closer for a shoulder to lean on. Kamala believes that if it were not for her family's help, she would not have excelled both as a lawyer and a politician. Remember that while others might leave your side during challenging times, your loved ones will never.

4. Don't Sit Around and Complain, Do Something!

Let's face it, it's either you choose to take action or continue complaining about things and not bother. During the Wilmington protest, Kamala thanked her mother for these wise words; "don't sit around and complain, do something." Every day she allows her mother's sentiments to inspire her daily tasks, which is why she is always winning.

5. Nothing can be more delightful than a smart joke.

Kamala's knack for humor helped her in winning hearts. Remember how she reacted to Donald Trump Jr.'s tweet mocking her laugh? The former president mocked her laugh and jokes as long and lame. Her response was just delightful, "You wouldn't know a joke if one raised you."

6. Her Executive Presence

Communicating as a leader is much more than what you say; it also includes your ability to dominate a room and make your presence known. Assessing how Harris makes a speech or speaks during an interview reveals that she effortlessly communicates with authority and elegance. She is not hesitant to allow her personality and femininity to shine through. Her vibrant personality, general friendliness, and captivating grin make her appear very approachable and trustworthy.

7. Connect Ambition With Purpose

As she stated in her memoir "The Truths We Hold: An American Journey," Harris's only goal was to be the solution, which saw her participating in bill formulation and change activism throughout her career. Although she got ridiculed following her rose to prominence, Harris is an example of why you should clarify your ambitions to drive you through your purpose.

8. Have a Voice To Stand for Your Values

There is no doubt that the US can feel Kamala's striking voice. She has been both an active writer and public speaker, even criticizing Trump's administration's failure to handle COVID-19 accordingly. She told the "New York Times" that when you're in a room with everyone expecting you to use your voice with pride and in a way that represents them, you realize how powerful your voice can be.

9. Flaunt Your Achievements

Harris introduced herself during the "Virtual Democratic National Convention" via her prosecutorial stories to familiarize herself with voters, highlighting her accomplishments in fighting gang and gang-related violence, sexual assault, and other issues. Women have been humbled as a result of patriarchy's consequences in order not to offend others. Like Harris, a little hot air is required to rise to get the job or any other role.

10. Show Your Vulnerability

As a leader, expressing vulnerability shows that you are also human. It also shows that you can relate to those listening to you. Harris does not shy off –of who she is and the challenges she faces.

Conclusion

Like Harris has demonstrated, be a leader that speaks up, chooses changes, stands your ground, and always acts with grace.

Chapter 26:
How To Stop Worrying About Failure

You and me, right now, right here, at this moment are in the best shape we could ever wish to be in. We are alive!

We think that we had a golden past, where we had everything. We had our parents to look out for us, we had friends to share our secrets with. We had a teacher to gossip about. Now It's just a load of responsibilities that we never wanted.

There is always an innate sense of fear in every human being, that He or she is going to fail at something they never wished to fail at. It's normal. But to give up to that fear is not natural, in fact, it is opposite to the very evolutionary trait of every Human Being.

The biggest myth we Humans have ever encountered is that if you stop doing something, you will never get the chance to fail at it. This is the wrong approach to life altogether. How many things can you avoid with this mindset?

Life is an album of events that will challenge you at every corner. You might fail at every other corner, but you will never fail at every single moment in life.

You have dreams you want to pursue, but you fear failing. The only motivation you need is to imagine the bigger image for when you finally get the chance to rise above all.

You don't need to think about what if you fail or what would people say if you never get what you struggled for. Even if you fail, you can walk away with your head held high because you stood for what you believed was right and what you deserved.

Living means doing the things you love to do. If you had to fall here and there to do what you want to achieve in life, then so be it.

Use your brain. Don't let your brain use you. Act like one unit. Don't let your body dictate your actions. Don't let your emotions derail you. Don't let the fear eat your confidence. It doesn't matter if you fail. You will get another chance to prove yourself. Even if you never succeed at a certain thing, there are countless things to achieve that you haven't thought of yet.

The ultimate failure is death itself. Every day you live is a success. Every second you breathe is a second you deserved. Every step you take towards your goal is a part of that success which will be your fate someday.

The best and the fastest way to deal with the fear of doing anything is to do it anyway.

You don't have to feel good to do things that you desire. It is just an illusion of your brain that tricks you and your body to waste yet another moment that could have been well spent.

Train your brain in a way that when you say I want to do this, Your brain never second guesses you. You start doing the thing in the tenth of a second.

It doesn't matter if you don't feel like doing it. Do it anyway. If you train yourself to act in this fashion, You will have the freedom, most people never have.

No man was ever born who had all the riches and never a glimpse of failure in their life. Every rich to ever exist also had a moment or years of struggle to achieve what they have today, but never did they second guess their instincts. Never did they let their fear get the best of them and then the world saw a new era on their hands.

The best advice I can give to buck up someone is simple but very deep; Follow your path no matter what trajectory it might take, just remember, fear the fear itself and you will rise like a phoenix.

Chapter 27:
How to Learn Faster

Remember the saying, "You are never too old to learn something new"? Believe me, it's not true in any way you understood it.

The most reliable time to learn something new was the time when you were growing up. That was the time when your brain was in its most hyperactive state and could absorb anything you had thrown at it.

You can still learn, but you would have to change your approach to learning.

You won't learn everything, because you don't like everything going on around you. You naturally have an ego to please. So what can you do to boost your learning? Let's simplify the process. When you decide to learn something, take a moment and ask yourself this; "Will this thing make my life better? Will this fulfill my dreams? Will I benefit from it?".

If you can answer all these questions in a positive, you will pounce on the thing and you won't find anyone more motivated than you.

Learning is your brain's capability to process things constructively. If you pick up a career, you won't find it hard to flourish if you are genuinely interested in that particular skill.

Whether it be sports, singing, entrepreneurship, cooking, writing, or anything you want to pursue. Just ask yourself, can you use it to increase your creativity, your passion, your satisfaction. If you can, you will start learning it as if you knew it all along.

Your next step to learning faster would be to improve and excel at what you already have. How can you do that? It's simple yet again!

Ask yourself another question, that; "Why must I do this? Why do I need this?" if you get to answer that, you will find the fastest and effective way to the top yourself without any coaching. Why will this happen on its own? Because now you have found a purpose for your craft and the destination is clear as the bright sun in the sky.

The last but the most important thing to have a head start on your journey of learning is the simplest of them all, but the hardest to opt for. The most important step is to start working towards things.

The flow of learning is from Head to Heart to Hands. You have thought of the things you want to do in your brain. Then you asked your heart if it satisfied you. Now it's time to put your hands to work.

You never learn until you get the chance to experience the world yourself. When you go through a certain event, your brain starts to process the outcomes that could have been, and your heart tells you to give it one more try. Here is the deciding moment. If you listen to your heart right away, you will get on a path of learning that you have never seen before.

What remains now is your will to do what you have decided. And when you get going, you will find the most useful resources immediately. Use your instincts and capitalize your time. Capture every chance with sheer will and belief as if this is your final moment for your dreams to come true.

It doesn't matter if you are not the ace in the pack, it doesn't matter if you are not in your peak physical shape, it doesn't matter if you don't have the money yet. You will someday get all those things only if you had the right skills and the right moment.

For all you know, this moment right now is the most worth it moment. So don't go fishing in other tanks when you have your own aquarium. That aquarium is your body, mind, and soul. All you need is to dive deep with sheer determination and the stars are your limit.

Chapter 28:
10 Habits of Taylor Swift

Well-versed pop star isn't the only description for the "American Sweetheart" Taylor Swift- She's a woman with many talents and abilities. As a world-famous singer-songwriter, accomplished businesswoman, and fitness guru, Swift has risen to become one of the world's most renowned celebrities.

She signed her first record deal at the age of 15, has been nominated for over 500 awards, has won 324, and has sold over 50 million albums. Such success did not simply land to her automatically. As per the new Netflix documentary Miss Americana, Swift's growth is a journey of countless disappointing and challenging life and career lessons.

Here are 10 habits of Taylor Swift that can enrich your life and career path.

1. Certainty

Getting to where you want to be in life credits a clear vision. With a sense of clarity, you can pave the way to reach that destination.

Since the day she started her career in music, Taylor Swift has been clear on what she wanted. From the very young age she has served to steer her decision making, and enjoyed every bit of it.

2. Focus on the Brighter Side

Taylor Swift has had a share of public scandals, tabloids exploitation, and people who aimed at tarnishing her name with controversy. It is irrelevant whether they are justified or not, she continues to produce and thrive in her positive space. Just like Taylor Swift, develop an urge to always working past the ruins while strengthening your optimistic moods.

3. You Have No Control Over What Happens

The incident at 2009 VMAs with Kanye West fuelled Swift's desire to prove that her talent is undeniable. You'll learn from the Concert's footage performing her most critically acclaimed song, "All Too Well", that she's was not up to changing what people would eventually say about her but was only concerned with respecting her work ethic. Make your response to criticism a reflection of respect for your hustle!

4. Credit Your Success to Having a Niche

In the entertainment business, and with successful people like Taylor Swift, each one has their unique niche/speciality that sets them apart from everyone else. Major deeply on what makes you unique and what brought you there as your storyline is only for you to tell.

5. Courage Is the Secret to Longevity

Taylor went from being a trial for sexual assault, which she won the case, to her mother ailing from breast cancer and brain tumour to all the publicized stunts she had been through. Despite the challenges, she managed to produce indisputably remarkable projects. Just like Taylor, your confidence, resilience, brilliance, work ethic, and steadfast trust in your process will definitely garner appreciation and respect.

6. Own Your Power

Taylor Swift not only has power, but she also owns it. Following Scooter Braun and Scott Borchetta incident, Taylor was not scared to jeopardize her image or face the consequences of speaking up against something she honestly believed was unfair.

There are always risks to speaking out, but sitting silence may be far riskier. In some circumstances, being silent may endanger your opportunity to manage a project or receive a promotion or increase.

7. Develop Your Support System

Nurture your relationships if you'd like to gain more influence. Even though you are not on the same scale as Taylor Swift, maintained friendships influences your world. Listen to them if you want them to listen to you.

8. Follow Your Heroes

Taylor Swift started her profession at a young age. Her childhood was fraught with difficulties but had motivation from her idols, whom she followed their advice. If you adore someone who influences your life path, emulating two or three things from them pays off.

9. Be Influential

Taylor's success in the music industry has been her driving force in influencing other people. You don't have to have her numbers to be impactful. When you devote your time and energy to becoming productive, influential stats and metrics will follow you.

10. Maintain a Healthy Lifestyle

Being a celebrity doesn't mean that Swift's healthy lifestyle is about trendy diets and strange eating habits that dominates the entire Hollywood culture. According to PopSugar, Swift eats salads, nutritious sandwiches, yoghurt and hit the gym regularly during the week.

Conclusion

You don't have to be Taylor Swift, but you can learn from her. Increase your influence, cultivate your network, develop credibility, wield your authority, focus on positivity, resilience is vital, and feel free to stand your ground as you work on your uniqueness.

Chapter 29:
6 Ways To Adopt A Better Lifestyle For Long-Term Success

A good lifestyle leads to a good life. The important choices we make throughout our lives impact our future in numerous ways. The need to make ourselves better in every aspect of life and the primary ability to perform such a routine can be a lifestyle. There is no proper way to live written in a book; however, through our shared knowledge and our comprehension, we can shape a lifestyle that can be beneficial and exciting at the same time. Though there is no doubt that falling into a specific routine can be difficult but, maintaining a proper state is more critical for a successful life.

For long-term success, a good lifestyle is a priority. Almost everything we do in our lives directly or indirectly involves our future self. So, a man needs to become habitual of such things that can profit him in every way possible. To visualize a better you, You need to configure just about everything around you. And to change all the habits that may make you feel lagging. The most common feature of a better lifestyle for long-term success is determination.

1. **Change In Pattern Of Your Life**

It is good to shape a pattern of living from the start and forming good habits, engaging yourself in profitable practice, and choosing a healthier custom. It feels impossible to change something you have already been habitual of, but willpower is the key. With some motivation and dedication, you can change yourself into a better version of yourself. You are choosing what might be suitable for you and staying determined on that thought. The first step is to let go of harmful things slowly because letting go of habits and patterns that you are used to can be challenging. After some, sometime you will notice yourself letting go of things more easily.

2. Take Your Time

Time is an essential factor when it comes to forming a lifestyle for a successful life. Time can seem to slow through the process, making us think that it may have been stopped in our most difficult moments. Similarly, making us feel it goes flying by when our life is relaxed and at ease. Time never stops for anyone. It is crucial to make sure we make most of our time and consume it in gaining more knowledge and power. Take time to inform your lifestyle, but not more than required. We are taking things at a moderate pace so you can both enjoy life and do work.

3. Don't Always Expect Things To Go Your Way

As much as we humans like to get our hopes high, we can't always expect things to go our way. Even things we have worked hard for can sometimes go downhill. It is at times overconfidence, but sometimes it can be pure bad luck. We can't get disheartened by something that was not meant to go a specific way. Don't expect perfection in all the work you do. Staying patient is the walk towards the reward. And making the best out of the worst can be the only way to get yourself going.

4. Don't Be Afraid To Ask For Help

It is human nature to ask each other for help now and then. If it comes to this point, don't be afraid to ask for help yourself. Ask someone superior to aid you on matters you find difficult. Don't hesitate to ask your inferiors who might have more knowledge than you in some certain customs. Help them, too, if needed. Ask them to assist you out on points, but never make them do the whole project. Don't make someone do something you wouldn't do yourself.

5. Be Prompt In Everything

Lagging behind your work can be the worst possible habit you could raise. Make yourself punctual in every aspect. Make sure you are on time everywhere. Either it's to wake up in the morning or to go to a meeting.

Laziness can never be proven good for you or your dream towards a prosperous lifestyle. Respect time, and it shall respect you. Show your colleges that they can depend on you to show up on time and take responsibility for work. You would rather wait than making others wait for you. That will show you seriousness toward your business.

6. Keep A Positive Attitude

Keeping a positive attitude can lead to a positive lifestyle. Be happy with yourself in every context, and make sure that everything you do has your complete confidence. Be thankful to all who surround you. Keep a positive attitude, whether it be a home or office. Speak with your superiors with respect and make yourself approachable around inferiors. Your positive mindset can affect others in a way too. They will become more inclined towards you, and they can easily suggest you help someone.

Conclusion

Just about everything in your life affects your future in a way or other, so make sure that you do all you can to make yourself worth the praise. Keep your lifestyle simple but effective. Try to do as much as possible for yourself and make time to relax as well. For long-term success, willpower is the most important; make sure you have it. Keep your headlight and calm for the upcoming difficulties and prepare yourself to face almost everything life throws at you.

Chapter 30:
5 Ways To Deal with Personal Feelings of Inferiority

Have you at some point felt that you are inferior to others? That's normal. All of us, at some point in our lives, have felt the same. Growing up, we saw other kids who performed better than us in the class. Kids who played sports well. Kids who were loved by all. We got jealous. We felt inferior to them. We constantly compared ourselves to them.

Almost everyone has experienced that in their childhood. But do you still feel the same about others? Do you constantly analyze situations and people around you? Do you feel worthless? Then you probably have an inferiority complex. But the good news is you can get over this inferiority complex. We are going to list some of the things that will help you in doing that.

1. **Build self-confidence**

Treat yourself better. Act confident. Do what you love. Embrace yourself. Is there anything in your body that you don't feel confident about? Maybe your smile, your nose, or your hair? The trick here is to either accept yourself the way you are or do something about it. If you have curly hair, get your hair straightener. Do whatever makes you feel better about yourself.

2. **Surround yourself with people who uplift you**

It's important to realize that your inferiority complex might be linked to the people around you. It might be your relatives, your friends at college, your siblings, or your colleagues. Analyze your interactions with them.

Once you can identify people who try to pull you down, do not reciprocate your feelings, or are not very encouraging, start distancing yourself from them. Look for positive people, who uplift you, and who bring out the better version of yourself. Take efforts to develop a relationship with them.

3. **Stop worrying about what other people think.**

One major cause of inferiority complexes is constantly thinking about what others are thinking about us. We seek validation from them for every action of ours. Sometimes we are thinking about their actions, while sometimes, we imagine what they think.

4. **Stop worrying about what other people think.**

One major cause of inferiority complexes is constantly thinking about what others are thinking about us. We seek validation from them for every action of ours. Sometimes we are thinking about their actions, while sometimes, we are imagining what they think.

Disassociate yourself from their judgments. It's ultimately your opinion about yourself that matters. When we feel good about ourselves, others feel good about ourselves.

5. Do not be harsh on yourself.

There is no need to be harsh on yourself. Practice self-care. Love yourself. Be kind to yourself. Do not over-analyze situations. Do not expect yourself to change overnight. Give yourself time to heal.

Chapter 31: Happy People View Problems as Challenges

To state the obvious: It's easier to be happy when things are going well. Positive outcomes are known to lift people's moods, while negative emotions (like anxiety) generally reflect concerns about negative outcomes.

But, happy people are also good at dealing with problems in ways that help them to maintain their mood, while still dealing with issues effectively. Here are three common things that happy people tend to do to deal with speed bumps in life.

FOCUS ON THE FUTURE

It is important to understand the problem you're facing, and so happy people certainly analyze the situation. But, they don't remain focused on the problem for long. That is, they avoid rumination—which is a set of repeated thoughts about something that has gone wrong.

Instead, they look to the future. There are two benefits to this: One is that the future is not determined yet, and so happy people can be optimistic about things to come. The other is that happy people are looking to make the future better than the past, which creates a hopeful outlook—no matter what the present circumstances look like.

FIND AGENCY

At any given moment, the situation you are in exerts some amount of control over your options. When you're sitting in traffic, for example, there isn't much you can do but wait for the cars around you to start moving. The amount of control you have to take action in a situation is your degree of agency.

Happy people seek out their sources of agency when problems arise. They are most interested in what they can do to influence the situation, rather than focusing on all of the options that have been closed off by what has happened. The focus on agency is important, because it provides the basis for creating a plan to solve the problem. And the sooner a problem is addressed, the less time it has to cause stress.

KNOW WHEN TO FOLD

There are always going to be big problems that you can't solve. Perhaps there is a client who is never satisfied with the work you do. Maybe there is a process you're trying to implement that never seems to have the desired outcome. You might even have been working on the problem for a long time.

Despite all the discussions about the importance of grit, effective (and happy) problem solvers are good at knowing when to walk away from a problem that can't be fixed. Each of us has a limited amount of time and energy that we can devote to the work we are doing. Spending time on problems that cannot be solved has an opportunity cost. There are other things you could be doing with your time that might yield better outcomes. It is important to learn when it is time to give up on a problem rather than continuing to try to solve it.

This is particularly true when you have been working on that problem for a long time. There is a tendency for people to pay attention to sunk costs—the time, money, and energy they have already devoted to working on something. But, those resources are gone, and you can't get them back. If it isn't likely that additional effort is going to help you solve a problem, then you should walk away, no matter how hard you have worked on it already. Happy people are good at ignoring those sunk costs both when making the decision to walk away from a project and after making the decision to walk away. They don't spend time regretting the "wasted" resources.

Chapter 32:
Why Are You Working So Hard

Your why,
your reason to get up in the morning,
the reason you act,
really is everything - for without it, there could be nothing.
Your why is the partner of your what,
that is what you want to achieve, your ultimate goal.
Your why will be what pushes you through the hard times on the path to your dreams.

It may be your children or a burning desire to help those less fortunate,
whatever the reason may be,
it is important to keep that in mind when faced with troubles or distractions.

Knowing what you want to do, and why you are doing it,
is of imperative importance for your life.
The tragedy is that most people are aiming for nothing.
They couldn't tell you why they are working in a certain field even if they tried.
Apart from the obvious financial payment,
They have no clue why they are there.

Is financial survival alone really a good motive to act?
Or would financial prosperity be guaranteed if you pursued greater personal preference?
Whatever your ambitions or preference in life,
make sure your why is important enough to you to guarantee your persistence.

Sometimes when pursuing a burning desire,
we can become distracted from the reason we are working.

Your why should be reflected in everything you do.
Once you convince yourself that your reason is important enough, you will not stop.
Despite the hardships, despite the fear, despite the loss and pain.
As long as you maintain a steady path of faith and resilience,
your work will soon start to pay off.
A light will protrude from the darkness and the illusionary troubles sent to test your faith will disappear as if they were never here.

Your why must be strong.
Your what must be as clear as the day is to you now.
And your faith must be eternal and unwavering.
Only then will the doors be opened to you.
This dream can be real, and will be.

When it is clear in the mind with faith, the world will move to show you the way.
The way will be revealed piece by piece, requiring you to take action and do the required work to bring your dream into reality.

Your why is so incredibly important.
The bigger your why, the greater the urgency, and the quicker your action will be.

Take the leap of faith.
Do what you didn't even know you could.
Never mind anyone else.
Taking the unknown path.
Perhaps against the advice of your family and friend,
But you know what your heart wants.

You know that even though the path will be dangerous, the reward will be tremendous.
The risks of not never finding out is too great.
The risk of never knowing if you could have done better is unfathomable.

You can always do better, and you must.

Knowing what is best for you may prove to be the most important thing for you.
How you feel about the work you are doing,
How you feel about the life you are living,
And how do you make the most of the time you have on this earth.
These may prove far more important than financial reward could ever do for you.

Aim to strike a balance.
A balance between working on what you are passionate about and building a wealthy financial life.
If your why and will are strong enough,
Success is all but guaranteed for you – no second guesses needed.

Aim for the sky,
However high you make it,
you will have proven you can indeed fly.

Chapter 33:
How Successful People Figure What To Focus On

Peak performance experts say things like, "You should focus. You need to eliminate the distractions. Commit to one thing and become great at that thing."

This is good advice. The more I study successful people from all walks of life—artists, athletes, entrepreneurs, scientists—the more I believe focus is a core factor of success. But there is a problem with this advice too.

Of the many options in front of you, how do you know what to focus on? How do you know where to direct your energy and attention? How do you determine the *one thing* that you should commit to doing? I don't claim to have all the answers, but let me share what I've learned so far.

MAKE A CALL ABOUT WHAT TO FOCUS ON

Assuming you're willing to try things and experiment a bit, the next question is, "How do I know what's coming easily to me?"

The best answer I can give is to pay attention. Usually, this means measuring something.

- If you're an entrepreneur, track your marketing and promotion efforts.

- If you're trying to gain muscle, track your workouts.

- If you're learning an instrument, track your practice sessions.

Even when you do measure things, however, there comes the point where you have to make a call and decide what to focus on.

In my mind, this moment of decision is one of the central tensions of entrepreneurship. Do we continue trying new things, or do we double down on one strategy? Do we try to innovate, or do we commit to doing one thing well?

Everyone wants to know the right time to simplify and focus on one thing, but nobody does. That's what makes success so hard. Entrepreneurship isn't like baking a cake. There is no recipe. There is no guidebook.

At this stage, your best option is to decide. You can't try everything. At some point, you don't need more information, and you just need to make a choice.

Now we have reached the stage where figuring out what to focus on becomes a real possibility. Welcome to the grind. It's time to put in a volume of work. Not just once or twice. Not just when it's easy. But a consistent, repeated volume of work. You have to fall in love with boredom and stay on the bus.

It is through this sheer number of repetitions that you'll come to understand the fundamentals of your task. You might know what greatness looks like before this point, but you won't understand how to achieve greatness until you've put the work in yourself.

GETTING TO SIMPLE

Now, finally, after trying many things and figuring out what to focus on, and putting in enough reps, you can begin to simplify. You can trim away the fat because you know what is essential and what is unnecessary.

As the Frenchman Blaise Pascal famously wrote in his Provincial Letters, "If I had more time, I would have written you a shorter letter."

Mastering the fundamentals is often the hardest and longest journey of all.

Chapter 34:
Becoming High Achievers

By becoming high achievers we become high off life, what better feeling is there than aiming for something you thought was unrealistic and then actually hitting that goal.
What better feeling is there than declaring we will do something against the perceived odds and then actually doing it.
To be a high achiever you must be a believer,
You must believe in yourself and believe that dream is possible for you.
It doesn't matter what anyone else thinks , as long as you believe,
To be a high achiever we must hunger to achieve.
To be an action taker.
Moving forward no matter what.
High achievers do not quit.
Keeping that vision in their minds eye until it becomes reality, no matter what.
Your biggest dream is protected by fear , loss and pain.
We must conquer all 3 of these impostors to walk through the door.
Not many do , most are still fighting fear and if they lose the battle, they quit.

Loss and pain are part of life.
Losses are hard on all of us.
Whether we lose possessions, whether we lose friends, whether we lose our jobs, or whether we lose family members.
Losing doesn't mean you have lost.
Losses are may be a tough pill to swallow, but they are essential because we cannot truly succeed until we fail.
We can't have the perfect relationship if we stay in a toxic one, and we can't have the life we desire until we make room by letting go of the old.

The 3 imposters that cause us so much terror are actually the first signs of our success. So walk through fear in courage , look at loss as an eventual gain, and know that the pain is part of the game and without it you would be weak.

Becoming a high achiever requires a single minded focus on your goal, full commitment and an unnatural amount of persistence and work.

We must define what high achievement means to us individually, set the bar high and accept nothing less.

The achievement should not be money as money is not our currency but a tool.

The real currency is time and your result is the time you get to experience the world's places and products , so the result should always be that.

The holiday home , the fast car and the lifestyle of being healthy and wealthy, those are merely motivations to work towards. Like Carrots on a stick.

High achievement is individual to all of us, it means different things to each of us,

But if we are going to go for it we might as well go all out for the life we want, should we not?

I don't think we beat the odds of 1 in 400 trillion to be born, just to settle for mediocrity, did we?

Being a high achiever is in your DNA , if you can beat the odds , you can beat anything.

It is all about self-belief and confidence, we must have the confidence to take the action required and often the risk.

Risk is difficult for people and it's a difficult tight rope to walk. The line between risk and recklessness is razor thin.

Taking risks feels unnatural, not surprisingly as we all grew up in a health and safety bubble with all advice pointing towards safe and secure ways.

But the reward is often in the risk and sometimes a leap of blind faith is required. This is what stops most of us - the fear of the unknown.

The truth is the path to success is foggy and we can only ever see one step ahead , we have to imagine the result and know it's somewhere down this foggy path and keep moving forward with our new life in mind.

Know that we can make it but be aware that along the path we will be met by fear , loss and pain and the bigger our goal the bigger these monsters will be.

The top achievers financially are fanatical about their work and often work 100+ hours per week.

Some often work day and night until a project is successful.

Being a high achiever requires giving more than what is expected, standing out for the high standard of your work because being known as number 1 in your field will pay you abundantly.

Being an innovator, thinking outside the box for better practices, creating superior products to your competition because quality is more rewarding than quantity.

Maximizing the quality of your products and services to give assurance to your customers that your company is the number 1 choice.

What can we do differently to bring a better result to the table and a better experience for our customers?

We must think about questions like that because change is inevitable and without thinking like that we get left behind, but if we keep asking that, we can successfully ride the wave of change straight to the beach of our desired results.

The route to your success is by making people happy because none of us can do anything alone, we must earn the money and to earn it we must make either our employers or employees and customers happy.

To engage in self-promotion and positive interaction with those around us, we must be polite and positive with everyone, even with our competition.

Because really the only competition is ourselves and that is all we should focus on.

Self-mastery, how can I do better than yesterday?

What can I do different today that will improve my circumstances for tomorrow.

Little changes add up to a big one.

The belief and persistence towards your desired results should be 100%, I will carry on until… is the right attitude.

We must declare to ourselves that we will do this , we don't yet know how but we know that we will.

Because high achievers like yourselves know that to make it you must endure and persist untill you win.

High achievers have an unnatural grit and thick skin , often doing what others won't, putting in the extra hours when others don't.

After you endure loss and conquer pain , the sky is the limit, and high achievers never settle until they are finished.

www.ingramcontent.com/pod-product-compliance
Lightning Source LLC
LaVergne TN
LVHW010347070526
838199LV00065B/5803